DIVING
BONAIRE

DIVING
BONAIRE

By George Lewbel and Larry Martin

AQUA QUEST PUBLICATIONS, INC. ■ NEW YORK

PUBLISHER'S NOTE

The Aqua Quest *Diving* series offers extensive information on dive sites as well as topside activities.

At the time of publication, the information contained in this book was determined to be as accurate and up-to-date as possible. The reader should bear in mind, however, that dive site terrain and landmarks change due to weather or construction. In addition, new dive shops, restaurants, hotels and stores can open and existing ones close. Telephone numbers are subject to change as are government regulations.

The publisher welcomes the reader's comments and assistance to help ensure the accuracy of future editions of this book.

Good diving and enjoy your stay!

Library of Congress Catalog Card Number: 91-071777

ISBN 0-9623389-4-X

This edition revised in April 1998.

Printed in Hong Kong

10 9 8 7 6 5 4 3 2

Cover: *A sharpnose puffer among orange cup corals. Photo: George Lewbel.*

Title page: *Trumpetfish often hide from their prey by swimming with larger fish, or blending into dense schools of smaller fish. Photo: Larry Martin.*

Facing foreword page: *Sea horses hide in staghorn coral thickets where it's difficult to see them. If you find one, please don't try to handle it. Sea horses are very delicate and may be killed by a careless squeeze. Photo: George Lewbel.*

ACKNOWLEDGEMENTS

We would like to thank the following for their assistance in the preparation of this book: Sally Sutherland Fosha, David E. Brannon, M.D., the Divi Flamingo Beach Resort and Casino, Dive Bonaire, Captain Don's Habitat, Photo Tours, Dee Scarr's Touch the Sea, the Sand Dollar Beach Club, Bruce Bowker's Carib Inn, Buddy Dive Resort, ALM Antillean Airlines, Sea Quest, Inc., and the Bonaire Tourist Bureau. We would especially like to thank David Serlin for sharing with us his knowledge and research.

For their assistance with the second edition, the authors thank Jack Chalk, Hugo Gerharts and Ronnie Pieters.

Thanks in advance to those divers who take time to write us, care of Aqua Quest Publications. We solicit your comments on this revised edition, and suggestions for the next.

Contents

FOREWORD   9

CHAPTER I

BONAIRE: *Diver's Paradise*   10

THE PAST
THE PRESENT
USEFUL INFORMATION
  *Climate ▪ Currency ▪ Electricity ▪ Entry & Exit
  Requirements ▪ Getting There ▪
  Island Etiquette ▪ Language ▪ Shopping ▪
  Telephone ▪ Time ▪ Transportation*

CHAPTER II

HOTELS & DIVE SHOPS   18

CHAPTER III

DINING: *Gourmet to Local Fare*   28

CHAPTER IV

DIVING   34

UNDERWATER TOPOGRAPHY
  Shelves ▪ Slopes ▪ Sand Flats
DIVE SITE IDENTIFICATION
WATER TEMPERATURE AND VISIBILITY
DEPTHS
MOORINGS
SHORE MARKERS
REEFS VS. DIVERS
  No Gloves ▪ Park Rules
BOAT DIVING
SHORE DIVING
SNORKELING
WINDWARD DIVING
REQUIRED SKILL LEVELS
EQUIPMENT
WARNING: BOAT TRAFFIC

CHAPTER **V**

DIVE SITES   44

LEEWARD BONAIRE   44

1. Lighthouse
2. Red Slave
3. Pink Beach
4. Salt City
5. Salt Pier
6. Jeanne's Glory
7. Alice in Wonderland
8. Angel City
9. *Hilma Hooker*
10. The Lake
11. Punt Vierkant
12. Debbie Bob
13. Chez Hines
14. Corporal Meiss
15. Windsock Steep
16. Calabas Reef
17. Town Pier
18. Something Special
19. Front Porch
20. Bari Reef
21. *La Machaca*
22. Cliff
23. Small Wall
24. Petrie's Pillar
25. Barcadera
26. Oil Slick Leap
27. Thousand Steps
28. Ol' Blue
29. Bloodlet
30. Rappel
31. La Dania's Leap
32. Karpata
33. Playa Bengé
34. Boca Bartól

KLEIN BONAIRE   74

35. Just-a-nice-dive
36. Bonaventure
37. Monte's Divi

38. Bonheur de Betsy
39. Joanne's Sunchi
40. Captain Don's Reef
41. South Bay
42. Hands-Off
43. Forest
44. Southwest Corner
45. Munk's Haven
46. Twixt
47. Sharon's Serenity
48. Valerie's Hill
49. Mi Dushi
50. Carl's Hill Annex
51. Carl's Hill
52. Jerry's Jam
53. Leonora's Reef
54. Knife
55. Sampler
56. Ebo's Reef

THE AUTHORS' FAVORITE SITES   92

57. RSD (Ricky-Sue-Dave)
58. Boca Dreifi (Chet's Cove)
59. Playa Frans

CHAPTER **VI**

MARINE LIFE   94

INVERTEBRATES   94
FISHES   112

APPENDIX **1**   125
EMERGENCY NUMBERS
DIVERS ALERT NETWORK

APPENDIX **2**   126
USEFUL NUMBERS FOR VISITORS

APPENDIX **3**   127
RESORTS AND SCUBA DIVING CENTERS

INDEX   130

FOREWORD

"Diver's Paradise" read the license plates on every vehicle in Bonaire, and for good reason, for Bonaire is the southern Caribbean's prime diving destination.

Surrounded by a spectacular fringe of living coral reefs teeming with an impressive array of tropical fishes, Bonaire and its little neighbor Klein Bonaire are blessed with an ideal mixture of sun, wind and rain. You can expect warm, clear water that is calm enough to be dived nearly every day of the year.

Bonaire has distinguished itself from most other Caribbean islands by making a serious, long-term commitment to preserving its coral reefs and fish life. Virtually the entire scuba zone is a protected marine park. No spearfishing or collecting has been permitted for years. In Bonaire, you can get eyeball-to-eyeball with marine animals that are rapidly being hunted to extinction on other islands.

This guidebook is the most extensive one available on Bonaire. It covers 59 dive sites on Bonaire and Klein, spanning a full range of scuba diving skills from novice through advanced. Sites that are particularly good for snorkelers are highlighted. There are descriptions of dives on coral reefs, piers, wrecks, gentle and steep slopes, and walls. For each site you will find information on depths, entries and exits, terrain, marine life, and photo tips, as well as special features of interest.

We have gone to great lengths to round out the diving portion of this guide with an array of detailed information on restaurants, resorts, dive operations and other topside activities to help you plan your vacation and make your stay on Bonaire more enjoyable. A special chapter on marine life offers a fascinating insight to the underwater world of Bonaire— both its vertebrates and invertebrates.

We hope you will enjoy this book as much as we have enjoyed writing it. Have fun, stay safe, and save a few tanks for us!

George Lewbel, Felton, California
Larry Martin, Galveston, Texas
April 1998

CHAPTER I

BONAIRE

Diver's Paradise

THE PAST

Bonaire's original inhabitants were the Arawak Indians whose cave paintings can still be seen today. The island was officially "discovered" in 1499 by Amerigo Vespucci sailing under the Spanish flag. The name Bonaire is said to have been derived from the Arawak word *bo-nah* meaning "low land."

Dominion over the Arawak Indians came in 1527 with the beginning of over a century of Spanish colonization. During their war of independence from Spain, the Dutch seized Bonaire in 1636. The Dutch East India Company soon formulated an economic plan for the island, emphasizing salt, corn and livestock production. Salt grew to be Bonaire's chief export by far, and the labor-intensive industry caused the demand for slaves to increase dramatically. The tiny stone huts where the slaves lived while working the salt pans can still be seen today on the southern part of the island.

The Dutch were under constant threat from British and French pirates in the early 1800's. The British seized Bonaire in 1800, lost it, and took it again in 1807. In 1816 the Dutch regained the island by treaty, and soon agriculture and salt production were flourishing. The abolition of slavery in 1863 made these operations uneconomical, resulting in the division and sale of many large landholdings. Drastically diminished trade over the subsequent years resulted in a lengthy depression of the economy.

Bonaire's fortunes rebounded dramatically in the early 1920's, as its workers found lucrative employment in the burgeoning oil industries of neighboring Curaçao and Aruba, where Shell and Standard Oil refined Venezuelan oil.

In the late 1950's, automation of the oil refining brought high unemployment back to the island. This period of recession was relatively brief, as the loss of off-island oil industry jobs was offset by government-supported revitalization of the salt industry, and by the development of tourism.

THE PRESENT

Bonaire is now part of the Netherlands Antilles, a self-governing part of the Netherlands. It is the second largest of the five Netherlands Antilles islands. The others are: Curaçao, St. Maarten, Saba, and St. Eustatius. Aruba withdrew from the group in January 1986 and is now an affiliated but independent political entity. Each island has a separate local government, but all participate in a single parliament (*de Staten*) concerning issues that affect all the islands.

Located 50 miles (80 km) north of Venezuela, Bonaire's surface area consists of 112 square miles (290 sq km). The island is 24 miles (37 km) long and 3–7 miles (5–11 km) wide. The highest elevation is Brandaris Hill (784 feet or 238 m). The hill provides an expansive view of the whole island and Klein Bonaire. Klein Bonaire, meaning "little" Bonaire, is an uninhabited islet located about 1/2 mile (.8 km) west of Bonaire. It is comprised of approximately 1500 acres (607 ha) of flat, rocky land with white sandy beaches.

Grey, yellow and red sponges flourish amidst orange cup corals on the pilings supporting the Town Pier. Photo Larry Martin.

The southern end of Bonaire is barely above sea level, and contains the salt flats. The arid land, covered with a tangle of scrub brush, cactus and aloe plants, gradually rises to a series of hills surrounding Brandaris in the Washington/Slagbaai National Park to the north. Mangroves thrive in areas of the east coast near the Lac Bay.

Bonaire's capital is Kralendijk, centrally located on the western shore. The island's population is about 11,000 people of Dutch, African and Indian descent.

In 1954, Bonaire's salt industry was modernized. Today, salt is the island's main export. It is shipped mostly to the United States, other islands of the Caribbean, and New Zealand. Other income-producing enterprises are the Bonaire Petroleum transfer terminal on the northwestern part of the island, and the radio towers of Trans World Radio and the Dutch World Broadcasting Co.

The mainstay of Bonaire's economy is tourism. About 27,000 divers a year visit the island's spectacular reefs. Bonaire has made a significant effort to maintain the high quality of its underwater world. The whole area surrounding the island to a depth of 200 feet (61 m) is a marine park where nothing may be taken or disturbed. All boats must use moorings within the park to prevent coral damage.

The wildlife preserve at Washington/Slagbaai National Park and the pink flamingo sanctuaries have contributed to the successful comeback of this interesting and unusual bird. Bonaire's commitment to its environment is clear.

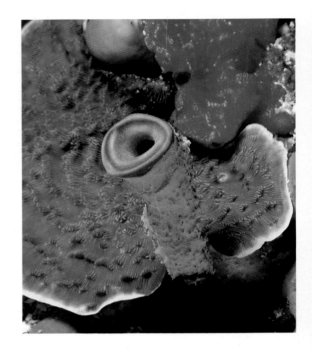

Two sponges compete for space with a saucer coral. Photo: George Lewbel.

The slave huts at Pink Beach stand as stark reminders of the former price of salt. Slaves working the salt pans slept in these hot little boxes along the beach. On their infrequent days off, they walked through the thorn-studded countryside to visit their families in Rincón and Antriol, near Kralendijk. They called their job site "White Hell."

The Capital: Kralendijk

Much of the island's history can be explored by walking through the capital city of Kralendijk (KRAH-len-dike). The town's layout enables you to walk from one end to the other in less than 15 minutes, passing many shops and historic buildings along the way.

Kralendijk, with a population of 1,500, has two main streets, Kaya Grandi and Kaya C.E.B. Hellmund. Besides the shops and stores, an interesting place to visit is the Plaza Reina Wilhelmina (Queen Wilhelmina Plaza).

Wilhelminaplein (Wilhelmina Park) marks the Plaza's center. Facing the sea, the tree and bench-lined Park is an excellent spot for a picnic lunch or to just people watch. It is said that Bonaire's yellow buildings, such as those surrounding the Park, received their color by order of a Netherlands Antilles Governor who was bothered by the glare of whitewash.

The Park is home to three historic monuments. A monument commemorating Dutchman Van van Welbeek's landing on Bonaire in 1634 stands in the center of the Park. Government House, built in 1832, was formerly the private residence of Bonaire's "Commander." A few steps away are the remains of historic Fort Oranje. Although the fort boasts over three hundred years of history, its cannons have never been used, except to offer salutes.

A stroll over to the town harbor brings you to the fish market, a small building styled like an ancient Greek temple, where Bonaireans purchase freshly-caught fish every morning.

The crown of a feather-duster worm trolls for organic particles and oxygen in the passing current. Photo: George Lewbel.

Hopefully, the concern Bonaire has shown in the past for nature will prevent the influx of divers and other tourists from having a negative impact on this diving mecca.

USEFUL INFORMATION

Climate. Bonaire is a desert island with a terrain and climate similar to southern Arizona. The average yearly temperature is 82 degrees Fahrenheit (28 degrees Celsius). Temperatures range from about 70-75°F (21-24°C) at night, and about 85-92°F (29-33°C) during the day. Due to the trade winds and moderate humidity, it rarely feels as hot as it is.

Rainfall is scant, consisting of a few brief showers in the early morning. During November and December, it can be overcast and rainy for a day or more. Total rainfall is about 20 inches (51 cm) per year, but every 8-10 years is a peak year with a total rainfall two or three times normal.

The sky is rarely completely clear over Bonaire. Usually it is dotted with puffy fair-weather clouds that give welcome respite from a tropical sun which can get quite intense at times, particularly in May, June and September.

Winds are always from the east at a brisk 15-20 mph (24-32 kph) from January through August. During the last four months of the year, wind velocity is lower with occasional calm days.

Currency. The legal currency is the Netherlands Antilles guilder, also called a *florin* and marked *FL* or *NaF* on signs and menus. On the street, $20 in U.S. currency is worth about 35 *NaF*. The exchange rate given by shops, hotels and banks varies from 1.75 to 1.80 *NaF* to the dollar.

Bank notes are issued in denominations of 5, 10, 25, 50, 100, 250 and 500 guilders. The guilder is divided into 100 cents. Coins are available in amounts of 1, 5, 10, 25 and 50 cents, and 1, and 2½ guilders. There are still some old smaller coins in circulation, so look carefully. The old nickels are square and make good souvenirs.

Nearly all businesses will accept U.S. paper currency and convert to the local currency. Except for a few major hotels, don't expect them to have U.S. currency to give back in change. Local banks and merchants have no mechanism for handling U.S. coins.

Major credit cards and traveler's checks are widely accepted. Local banks charge merchants a fee to cash traveler's checks or honor credit cards, so some merchants will pass this cost on to you.

Electricity. Wall outlets supply 127 and/or 220 volts AC, 50 Hz. Most dive operations have an electrical strip with transformers to allow semi-safe charging of batteries for lights and strobes, but keep your eye on them. Chargers do tend to overheat.

Entry and Exit Requirements. While a passport is not required, U.S. and Canadian citizens need proof of identity and a return or continuing ticket. For Americans, a birth or naturalization certificate, alien registration card or voter's registration card are acceptable. For Canadians, an I.D. card or birth certificate will do. There is a $10 exit tax collected at the airport before departure. This information may be subject to change, so be sure to check before your trip.

Getting There. From North America, Bonaire is served by ALM, the national airline of the Netherlands Antilles. The pilots are good, the planes are clean and comfortable, the meals are quite good, and the drinks are free. ALM currently offers direct flights to Bonaire from Atlanta on Saturdays, and from Miami on Wednesdays and Saturdays. You can also fly ALM to Curaçao or Aruba, but you should expect some airport delays in getting to Bonaire on the ALM inter-island flights. Air Aruba and Avensa also service the islands. Check with your travel agent for current information.

If you are connecting through Miami, it might be wise to check your bags to Miami and deliver them yourself to the ALM counter, if you have a few hours to make the connection. Most of the lost or delayed baggage problems can be traced to slow airport baggage handling.

Island Etiquette. The people of Bonaire are some of the most friendly you will meet anywhere in the world. North Americans, particularly from the big cities, are so calloused by the day-to-day hostility they must deal with that they often react with suspicion to this warmth. Many suspect they are being set up for some kind of scam. The Bonairean on the street whom you are sure you have never met before really is wishing you a sincere "Good Morning" simply as one human being to another, and probably has no ulterior motive whatsoever.

Greetings are very important in Bonairean culture, and it is essential to return them when offered, whether you think you know the person or not. The Bonairean equivalent of announcing that a state of war exists between one's self and another person is to say "He is not greeting me." If someone waves or toots a horn, wave back. Initiate all conversations or transactions with a greeting appropriate to the time of day. Many Bonaireans, particularly in the tourist industry, have given up greeting North Americans since they have discovered that many of them are very rude people who only stare back coldly when offered a normal pleasant greeting. Help correct this image.

Bonaireans are fairly conservative by nature, and the older ones in particular find the wearing of bathing attire on the street quite offensive. On the beach or boat, or walking around at the resort, bikinis and other brief clothing are just fine. European women even go topless on some beaches. But if you are going into town or just walking from resort to resort along the road, pull on shorts and a shirt to avoid getting some people upset.

If you are planning on going to one of the more formal restaurants in town, transacting any banking or other business, or meeting with any government officials while on the island, slightly more formal attire is needed. Men should wear long pants, shoes and a collared shirt, and women should have dresses. While some government people wear ties to work, no one else ever wears them except for services at some churches.

Language. Most Bonaireans need to be linguistic gymnasts to get around. The mother tongue of most of the residents—and the language most spoken in homes and on the street—is a Portuguese-based Creole called Papiamento. The "official" language of the island is Dutch. Dutch is used by all the schools, governmental agencies and larger businesses. The radio blasts mostly rapid-fire Spanish from nearby Venezuelan stations, and the tourist industry works almost entirely in English.

Bonaire's candle cacti are well protected by thorns. Locals carry chunks of cactus about with special (long!) tongs, and cultivate them as fences to keep goats and other intruders out of their gardens. Be careful when hiking; fragments of these cacti litter the ground in many areas. Photo: Dave Brannon.

SIGHTSEEING ON BONAIRE

Plan on spending some time exploring Bonaire topside as well as underwater. Two half-days—one in the north and one in the south—is enough time to visit most sights of interest on the island.

There are two ways to tour Bonaire. First, you can rent a car, pack your dive gear and dive the southern or northern sites visiting points of interest along the way.

Second, you can use the services of **Bonaire Tours**, who will pick you up at your hotel in an air-conditioned vehicle and provide you with a knowledgeable tour guide. Bonaire Tours offers several packages. The half-day southern tour visits the salt pans, slave huts, Willemstoren Lighthouse, flamingo sanctuary and Lac Bay. The half-day northern tour visits 1000 steps, Goto Lake, Rincón, Arawak Indian inscriptions, and an observation point with an excellent view of both Bonaire and Klein Bonaire. There are several other packages available including an extended tour of Washington/Slagbaai National Park. Bonaire Tours can be reached at 8300.

Purple tube sponges abound at many of Bonaire's dive sites. Photo: George Lewbel.

The aloe plant's leaves contain a sticky, gelatinous fluid that many people believe to be medicinal. Aloe is harvested commercially for use in sunburn preparations. Torn open and placed on irritated skin, an aloe leaf seems to ease the pain. Very large aloe plantations were first established on Bonaire around 1840, and their remnants can still be seen in Washington/Slagbaai National Park.

Nearly all Bonaireans understand some spoken English and many can speak it surprisingly well, particularly considering that it is the third or fourth language they learn. It is an extraordinary commentary on the importance of North American tourism to the island's economy that so many of the signs in the airport, on businesses in town and even the license plates are in English, a language not everyone can read easily.

Shopping. Almost all the shops on Bonaire are clustered along the few main streets near the Town Pier in the capital of Kralendijk. The town is so small that you can walk from one side to the other along the main street, Kaya Grandi, in about 10 minutes.

The Capitol's shopping area features quaint shops in colorfully painted buildings. It is here that native Bonaireans do their daily shopping. Although many stores are geared toward the tourist trade, several stores such as Casa Pana (the island's oldest general store), carry items of necessity. Besides the usual boutiques offering tee shirts, souvenirs and clothing, there are jewelry and perfume stores, as well as some selling wood and leather goods. Pick up a copy of *Bonaire Holiday*, a free tourist handout which has advertisements from most of the major stores and a map with their locations.

Most shops are open from 8 A.M. to noon and from 2 P.M. to 6 P.M. Monday through Saturday. From noon to 2 P.M. is siesta time.

Telephone. Direct dialing to many countries including the United States and Canada is available. To dial directly to Bonaire from the United States, use 011–599–7 plus the four-digit local number. Be patient. It sometimes takes hours to call home.

Time. Bonaire is in the Atlantic Standard Time Zone, one hour ahead of Eastern Standard Time. Daylight Savings Time is not observed.

Transportation. The dive operations located in hotels all have boats to run trips along the Bonaire coast and to Klein Bonaire. Though they do run trips to some of the very distant southern and northern sites, most do so on an irregular basis

There are plenty of car rental agencies in town and rentals can be arranged through your hotel. You will need a valid driver's license and proof of your ability to pay for possible damages. A major credit card will do. Road signs are in kilometers and international symbols are used. Driving is on the right. There may be some restrictions on driving rental cars along the rugged dirt roads in Washington/Slagbaai Park. Be sure to ask first. Vans and trucks are sometimes available for rental.

Even if you don't need a car to go diving, there is a lot to see on the island, such as the salt works, slave huts, flamingos, Arawak Indian cave paintings and the Park. Unless you take a tour bus, a rental car is the only economical way to get around for long distances. Taxis are available for shorter runs.

CHAPTER **II**   HOTELS & DIVE CENTERS

We have included here brief descriptions of resorts that are of specific interest to divers in order to give you a feeling for the atmosphere there. Before deciding on where to stay, consult your local dive center or travel agency who can provide you with additional detailed information, including changes since this section was updated.

Except for some very expensive resorts, all the hotels and condo units seem roughly competitive in price, and most have excellent dive operations on site or close by. Where you stay should depend mostly on how many people you are traveling with and what kind of ambiance you like during a vacation. There are frenetic party places, quiet getaways, and even secluded private houses overlooking the water with excellent diving only yards from your back porch.

If you are traveling as a family or with a small group of friends, your options really expand, since many of the villas and condo units on the island rent for a flat daily fee. These prices may seem steep until you divide them among the people sharing the unit. In this way you can obtain private luxury accommodations for less that the cost of a small hotel room. Condos and villas usually come with fully-equipped kitchens. You can save a great deal of money fixing some of your own meals and buying drinks by the case at the market.

STOCKING THE PANTRY

Though a lot cheaper than restaurant meals, much store-bought food will seem very expensive by North American standards. Except for local fish, nearly all food has to be flown in or shipped to the island in refrigerated containers. Below is a sampling of where to look for groceries on the island.

Sand Dollar Groceries

This store is located at the Sand Dollar Beach Club complex, one mile (1.6 km) north of town. It is an American-style convenience store and deli that is extremely well stocked by local standards.

Cultimara Supermarket

For smaller quantities of canned food, soda, juice, liquor, beer or bug spray, this place in the center of Kralendijk has the best prices. Stocking levels vary drastically depending on when the last container ship arrived. They are closed midday, evenings and Sundays. Fresh foods such as bread, milk, meat, fish or produce are better bought elsewhere. There is another market next door with good fresh food, but higher prices on most other items.

Orange ball anemones are very sensitive to bright lights, and are never seen exposed in the daytime. At night, look under ledges, especially near the sandy bases of coral heads. Keep your dive light partially covered when you find one, or it will retract its tentacles and withdraw into a hole. This individual was found on one of the large cement pylons at the Town Pier. Orange ball anemones aren't really anemones, although they are closely related. They are actually corallimorpharians, meaning "coral-shaped animals," sometimes called false corals. Photo: Dave Brannon.

Plate corals growing at the base of a gorgonian sea fan. Photo: George Lewbel.

Exito Bakery

Delicious baked goods are available here. The French bread is often still so hot from the oven that it has to be handled with tongs. Excito is in the center of town just west of Cultimara. They also have a small selection of produce and preserved meats.

Venezuelan Fruit Boats

What used to be the local fish market in the harbor is now occupied by entrepreneurs who sail over from Venezuela every week and set up an open-air shop. You can find some real bargains here on seasonal produce. Depending on the month, you can get limes, watermelons, huge papayas, mangoes and avocados. The oranges look bad but are great juicers. Prices are reasonable but seldom is English spoken. Just point at what you want and the proprietor will use sign language to indicate the price.

FIFOCO, M.B.F. and CONSALES

These three large warehouses are all located on Kaya Industria, where there is a miniature industrial park. It is easy to find; it dead-ends into the Flamingo Beach Resort's tennis courts. Here is where the hotels, restaurants and grocery stores buy their food. Although most business done here is wholesale, they will sell retail and will even break case lots on some items. Best buys on wine and spirits are at CONSALES, while across the street at FIFOCO, you can get a wide range of frozen foods including meat, seafood and produce.

FIFOCO sometimes has fresh produce (leaf lettuce and herbs) that is unavailable anyplace else. M.B.F. (with the picture of a large Maine lobster on the building) imports frozen fish, shrimp and North Atlantic lobster meat, but you have to buy it in large quantities.

Fresh Fish

The best buys on locally caught fresh fish are usually from individual fishermen or middlemen who distribute the day's catch to the locals. The Bonairean dive guides at your dive shop will know where to find someone willing to sell you a wahoo, dorado or some deep water snappers. You'd be smart to bring the guide along to help you find the correct house, and to negotiate the transaction. Though the guide will be happy to help you out just for fun, it would be good Bonairean manners to offer the guide a small non-cash gift such as a piece of the fish you buy in recognition of his assistance.

RESORTS

The first telephone number given is the local number on Bonaire. To dial directly from the United States, precede the four-digit local number with **011-599-7**. The second number is the resort's representative in the United States.

Black Durgon Inn   8978

The Black Durgon, located north of Habitat, is a small inn with nine rooms, two villas and three apartments. The villas have fully-equipped kitchens. Bedrooms are air-conditioned, but modest compared to most of the other resorts on the island. An informal American-style breakfast is the only meal served, although the open air kitchen is available for guests' use. "Dine around" meal packages allow guests to use a variety of restaurants on the island for their other meals.

Black Durgon reservations are offered exclusively through dive shops. The place has a loyal following of those who are in Bonaire solely for diving and are not interested in any luxuries.

Diving at the Black Durgon

The Black Durgon is home of the Bonaire Scuba Center, run by American Al Catafumo and Bonairean Eddy Statia. Good beach diving is available directly off the beach at Small Wall.

Because of the size of the operation, they can put together custom dive packages to cater

to their clients' wishes. Overland "dive safaris" can be arranged to southern sites and northern sites in the Park. When conditions are right, trips are also made to the windward side of the island.

Buddy Beach & Dive Resort   5080
                                (800) 359-0747

Located between the Sand Dollar and the Habitat, the Buddy Beach & Dive Resort has 40 rooms some with kitchenettes. The resort has its own restaurant and a freshwater pool seaside of the rooms, with a poolside bar. Buddy's has traditionally been popular with Europeans.

Diving at Buddy Beach & Dive Resort

Buddy Dive, a 5-star PADI facility, provides basic and advanced training in French, German, Spanish and English. Gear storage is available, and gear and tanks may be taken 24 hours a day. The resort owns several vehicles for shore diving excursions. Personally-guided dives are also available.

Captain Don's Habitat   8290
                                (800) 327-6709

Captain Don Stewart originally arrived on Bonaire aboard his sailboat, *Valerie Queen*, about 30 years ago. He started Habitat to cater to the hardcore diver who was interested only in spending as much time underwater as possible, and saw no point in spending a lot of money for the services of a fancy resort hotel. Captain Don was the first dive operator on Bonaire.

Much has changed since those early days. Captain Don is still a host several nights a week in the bar area, but now spends most of his time practicing horticulture on his farm. Ask him about the luxurious plantings surrounding the Habitat.

A lot of money has now been pumped into the resort, which now has 93 units. The hardcore "monk cells" have been completely refurbished into two-bedroom cottages with living rooms, kitchens and patios. While they do not have an ocean view, they do face a lush tropical garden.

Two-story villas on the north side of the

resort are available in various configurations. Most have large oceanfront rooms, private balconies and refrigerators. The second floor suites command a sweeping vision of the sea, Klein Bonaire and sunsets.

The deluxe junior suites, just south of the restaurant area, live up to their name. They are very pleasant and all have a spectacular view of the sea and Klein Bonaire. They are also more convenient than the villas, with easier parking and instant backdoor access to the new pool and hot tub. The informal restaurant, Rum Runners, offers three meals a day at moderate prices. The thatch-roofed bar is a great place for toasting the sunset.

Diving at the Habitat

Habitat bills itself as the home of "Diving Freedom" and indeed air, gear and very good shore diving are all available 24 hours a day with no advance planning.

Habitat is a PADI 5-star training and instructor development facility, a NAUI "dream destination" and an SSI referral and instructor development center. In addition to open water and advanced certification, Habitat offers courses through instructor level. Over 20 specialty courses are also taught. A one week photography seminar is also available.

Habitat's dive boats visit all of Klein Bonaire as well as the Washington Park sites.

Carib Inn   8819

Bruce Bowker has been running this very small, very quiet and impeccably managed operation for over a decade. Located just a few feet south of the Divi Flamingo Beach Resort, the Carib Inn is a serene oasis. It may be too quiet for some people, but many divers would stay nowhere else. Over 60 percent of his customers are returning guests. Bruce's operation has grown very slowly, and he has avoided the temptation to expand to the point where he can't oversee every detail himself.

The Carib Inn has only thirteen rooms, seven with full kitchens. Four of the rooms are clustered around a small freshwater pool and four overlook the sea. In keeping with Bruce's approach that his guests are just that, personal guests, none of the rooms are numbered.

Diving at the Carib Inn

The Carib Inn's dive operation has been considered for years to be one of the best run on the island. All levels of PADI instruction are offered in English. The dock and dive boats are just 50 feet (15 m) from the rooms.

The Inn's customers tend to be very serious about their diving. The boats leave earlier in both the morning and afternoon than at other resorts to insure that they have their pick of the reefs. Normally, there are fewer than 10 divers in the boat accompanied by Bruce or one of the other instructors on staff.

Certified divers are expected to take responsibility for their own diving. Anyone asking for guidance will get it, but otherwise, you are free to dive as you please provided you don't endanger other divers, the divemaster, or the marine environment with your actions.

Divi Flamingo Beach Resort   8285
                                    (800) 367-3484

The Divi Flamingo consistently gets good reviews. While it tends to have a bit of a "let's party" atmosphere, that is exactly why a lot of the guests stay here. There are tennis courts, two bars, two pools, a hot tub and a casino at the Flamingo. There are also two restaurants— the informal Calabas Terrace and the more formal three-tiered Chibi Chibi.

The Flamingo has 145 rooms, including some with access for wheelchairs. The best of the hotel's rooms, at least for divers, are probably 205-212 and 116-124. They overlook the water, and are close to the dive shop.

Diving at the Divi Flamingo

The dive operation at the Flamingo is huge. It employs over 30 workers and operates from two large piers simultaneously. At peak periods, Peter Hughes Dive Bonaire is host to over 200 divers at a time.

Dive Bonaire's instructional department has two large air-conditioned classrooms. NAUI, PADI and SSI classes are taught in English, Dutch, Spanish and German, and include many specialties as well as open water through instructor. A complete line of scuba equipment is available for rental. Nikonos cameras can be rented, bought or serviced and E-6 processing is available.

Dive Bonaire owns numerous boats, which leave in the morning and afternoon from both docks. There is a boat night dive available every night except Saturday. Tanks and gear are available between 8:00 A.M. and 5 P.M. except some nights when the center is open until 9 P.M. If you want to dive earlier or later than that, you must take your own personal equipment and tanks to your room.

Harbour Village Beach Resort   7500
(800) 424-0004

The Harbour Village Beach Resort, along a quarter mile (.4 k) of white sand beach, is one of the most luxurious facilities on the island. The 70 air-conditioned rooms include one- and two-bedroom suites, and feature cool white tiled floors, ceiling fans, televisions, showers and French doors that lead to patios or terraces. The resort is located on a landscaped peninsula on the ocean side of the marina north of town.

A blackbar soldierfish peeks out from beneath a head of boulder star coral. As one of the bolder members of the squirrelfish family, the blackbar is often seen in the daytime next to coral heads. Most others hide deep in coral crevices until nightfall. Photo: Larry Martin.

The 60-slip marina, which is owned by the Harbour Village, is the only facility of its kind on the island, and can accommodate vessels from the smallest day cruiser to a large oceangoing yacht. The resort offers an extensive selection of sailing and fishing rentals and charters.

The Kasa Coral restaurant overlooks the pool and has an international menu for intimate dining. It is adjacent to a cocktail lounge and piano bar with live music. The more casual La Balandra Bar & Grill serves luncheon beachside, and is open for happy hour and after dinner drinks. Captain's Walk, the newest restaurant is located by the marina.

Other facilities include a freshwater pool, tennis courts, aerobics instruction, and a "European Spa" with a full range of diet and exercise options.

Water sports, other than diving include sailing, kayaking and windsurfing.

Diving at the Harbour Village

The dive shop at Harbour Village is Great Adventures Bonaire. Besides morning and afternoon dives, there is usually one night dive per week depending on demand.

PADI and NAUI courses are offered from openwater to divemaster, and are taught in English, Dutch, German and Spanish.

The shop is closed from noon until about 1:30 P.M. Tanks, buoyancy compensators and regulators are available for rental. There are storage lockers for dive gear.

Lions Dive Hotel Bonaire   5580
(800) 786-3483

Located next to Captain Don's Habitat, the Lions Dive Hotel has 31 one- and two-bedroom oceanfront suites featuring fully equipped kitchens, air-conditioning, television, telephones and private balconies or patios. The kitchens include microwave ovens and utensils. Living rooms have sofas that pull out to queen size beds. There is a large freshwater pool with sun decks.

Diving at the Lions Dive Hotel

Bon Bini Divers runs the dive operation and offers certifications from open water to assistant instructor through PADI or CMAS. In addition over 20 specialty courses, including photography, are offered.

Dive boats depart in the morning and afternoon with two night dive boat trips weekly. Shore diving is available 24 hours a day. Gear storage for guests is located on the dock and can be accessed at any time.

Sand Dollar Beach Club   8738
(800) 288-4773

This complex is located on the shore, just a short stroll north of the Sunset Beach Hotel. The Sand Dollar is one of the finest places to stay, dive and eat on the island.

Its two-story buildings zigzag down the coast in a large "W" shape with spacious gardens and walkways between them. Because the restaurant and dive center are built on a platform at the base of the cliff, the view of the sea from the condos is unobstructed, even from the ground floors.

Condo units are available as studios, one-, two- and three-bedroom units. The rooms are tiled, and furnished with modern rattan and glass furniture manufactured locally. Televisions with cable stations, and ceiling fans are also included. All units come with a full bathroom for each bedroom. The living rooms have convertible sofas, so a three-bedroom unit could hold six or eight people, making the per person cost reasonable even in high season.

Kitchens are fully equipped, and the Sand Dollar has its own grocery store close by. The complex is also served by The Green Parrot Restaurant, one of the best informal eating places on the island.

In the sea in front of the complex, there are floating rafts equipped with pool ladders. On the other side of the condos is a large freshwater pool and two lighted tennis courts.

Diving at the Sand Dollar

The Sand Dollar Dive and Photo Center, managed by Andre and Gabrielle Nahr, is first class all the way, with some of the best-trained staff on the island.

Though most of Andre's effort is now spent in managing the diving operation, he is an experienced PADI and NAUI instructor who can teach in any of five languages. Sand Dollar is a PADI 5-star training facility and instructor development center.

All the instructors are cross certified with both NAUI and PADI, and they hold many specialty ratings. This is an excellent place to learn to dive or to upgrade your skills.

Tanks are available 24 hours a day. Personal dive gear stored at the dock can be accessed until about 10:00 each night. Divers wishing to dive later than that need to remember to transfer their personal gear from the main gear storage area to the small individual gear lockers outside for which keys may be borrowed during business hours.

Boats go out promptly for morning and afternoon dives with a night boat dive scheduled for Wednesdays.

Smaller boats are available for small groups or photo excursions. They are equipped with special photo setup tables and rinse tanks.

A fully equipped and newly expanded photo shop is on site with same day E-6 processing, numerous work tables, light tables, projectors and video monitors available for viewing the day's results. The Sand Dollar stocks a complete line of diving, photo and video equipment for both rent or sale.

Sunset Beach Hotel 8291
(800) 328-2288

The Sunset Beach Hotel is located on a wide expanse of white sand beach that slopes gently into the water.

The hotel makes good use of the beach— water sports include water skiing, windsurfing, water scooters, glass bottom paddle boats, and small sailboats.

The hotel's 145 rooms each have a television and telephone, not at all typical for this part of the world. Standard rooms are on the ground floor and face east, away from the water. Superior rooms have a garden view. Only the second floor deluxe rooms give a clear view of the sea. Hardcore divers will want to ask for numbers 119-124 or 216-221, which are closest to both the dive shop and the back parking lot, facilitating quick transfer of

gear for both shore and boat excursions.

The Playa Lechi, commonly called the Beach Hut, is a scenic open air restaurant with a thatched roof right on the beach. On the beach side of the restaurant is a very popular long wooden bar staffed by an experienced and able crew of Bonaireans. A second restaurant, the Sunset Terrace, is popular for its theme nights.

The Sunset Beach Hotel is a good choice for couples, families, or dive groups who are looking for large, quiet surroundings, and who are not interested in doing any of their own cooking. Nondivers will enjoy the hotel's tennis, beach volleyball, miniature golf, surface water sports and sunbathing.

Diving at the Sunset Beach

The Sunset Beach Dive Center, a PADI 5-star facility operated by Anton van den Heetkamp, is located at the south end of the beach. Anton is an experienced instructor who was the chief technician for the hospital's hyperbaric chamber. For those wishing to learn to dive or upgrade their skills, PADI instruction is provided, including a number of specialty courses.

Tanks and gear are available during business hours. Night divers may make arrangements to get tanks after hours. There are two boat dives scheduled in the morning and two in the afternoon. Those divers who like to sleep in or take a late lunch can catch the late morning or late afternoon trip. Night boat dives will be run on request.

Sunset Inn/Sunset Villas/Sunset Diversion/
Sunset Hamlet Villas 8291/8448
(800) 344-4439

These properties have names similar to the Sunset Beach Hotel because they are all owned by the same company.

The Sunset Inn, located along the water in downtown Kralendijk is a small seven-room facility that is suitable mainly for European students and others on tight budgets. The Inn is adjacent to the Dive Inn (run by Anton and Babs van den Heetkamp) so good diving and equipment is readily available. Babs runs the Dive Inn operation, while Anton now spends

are not overly interesting for divers. Others are in spectacular scenic settings and are good values for a family or a small group.

One of the very nicest of these, particularly for groups with children or nondivers, would be the flagship property: The Sunset Beach Villa. Formerly the manager's house for the government hotel, this three-bedroom, two-bath house sits at the end of Sunset Beach Hotel's giant waterfront area. Open the backyard gate and you're standing on the sand, 50 feet (15 m) from the dive shop. It has a well-equipped kitchen that includes a microwave. If three couples share the expense, it is a bargain during the high season, considering what you get.

Other houses are located in an upscale, quiet secluded area south of the airport called Belnem. They are all perched on a ledge overlooking the water near some excellent diving and snorkeling. "Belnem Number 90" is Peter Hughes' former mansion. It is a very beautiful three-bedroom house with a free-standing glassed-in gourmet kitchen and a view that will make you want to stay forever. It is a real bargain even during peak season if shared by three couples.

People staying at these properties may arrange diving through any operator on the island, though packages bought in advance will usually be booked with the Dive Inn operation.

Plaza Resort Bonaire   2500
(800) 766-6016

The Plaza, located a half mile from the airport, is the largest resort on Bonaire with 200 suites and villas, all with air-conditioning, cable TV, telephones and kitchens. For those not wanting to cook their own meals there are three restaurants. One is the Banana Tree on ocean front which serves island dishes in an informal setting. For French and Caribbean dishes in a more formal setting, try the Caribbean Point. There is also a Mexican restaurant. The resort's three bars offer drinks, snacks and entertainment. A swimming pool, fitness center, sandy beach and an onsite casino offer additional amenities.

Besides scuba, there are plenty of watersports at the Plaza including aqua

Many water sports besides diving are available in Bonaire. This couple is taking advantage of the fine beach at the Sunset Beach Hotel to study their open water diver manuals.

most of his time operating the Sunset Beach Dive Center.

The Sunset Villas are former private houses that have been bought and completely furnished, and now rent by the night or by the week. Some of these are located in town and

Sheet corals usually grow largest in deep water, where they spread out to catch the limited amount of light there. Because they are below most wave action, they don't need to grow heavy skeletons, but rather form stacks of thin, fragile plates. They are often difficult to identify to species, especially without close-up photographs. This colony is probably either Lamarck's (Agaricia lamarcki) or Graham's (A. grahamae) sheet coral. Photo: Larry Martin.

jogging, banana boat rides, windsurfing, kayaking and water-skiing.

Diving at the Plaza Resort

Toucan Diving is the resort's on-premises dive operation. They teach PADI and NAUI courses, and IDD (Dutch certification) through instructor. Classes are taught in English, Dutch, German and Spanish. Rental gear is TUSA and

there is individual gear storage available. E-6 developing, camera rental and specialty courses are also available.

Daily boat schedules are flexible and depend on the number of divers. One weekly night dive is scheduled, but more are available on request as are shore trips to Washington Park and the east coast. Shore diving is available 24 hours a day.

CHAPTER **III** DINING

Gourmet to Local Fare

RESTAURANTS

If you categorize restaurants by style instead of by cuisine, there are basically three kinds of places to eat on Bonaire. There are formal restaurants, with fancy decor, gourmet cooking, and high prices. There are informal restaurants where shorts and tee shirts are welcome, and which are often open air and breezy. Then there are local snack bars that would be the equivalent of fast food joints, except that nothing involving food is particularly fast in Bonaire.

There are about 20 restaurants in the Kralendijk area, including those at the hotels. Many cater primarily to tourists and the few wealthy expatriates and island residents who can afford them. Others have a mixed local and tourist clientele. Still others are patronized only by residents and the rare adventuresome tourist who is willing to overlook appearances for new taste experiences.

At all the following recommended establishments, if you have a comment about the food or service, you shouldn't have to go far to tell someone. One of the owners is either the waiter, the busboy or the bartender, and sometimes all three.

Beefeater Restaurant   7776

Located in a typical Bonairean town house on Kaya Grandi in Kralendijk, the Beefeater is one of the oldest quality restaurants on the island. Fresh fish and steak dishes dominate the menu. The restaurant is air-conditioned and has an intimate bar. Open for dinner every day except on Sundays. Reservations recommended.

China Garden   8480

If you have a craving for Chinese food, try the China Garden Bar and Restaurant on Kaya Grandi in Kralendijk. Home to the only authentic Chinese stove in the Antilles, China Garden serves Chinese, Indonesian and western specialties in a restored Bonairean mansion. Curried chicken or shrimp, Indonesian *nasi* and *bami goreng*, fresh seafood, and steaks are some of the offerings of this air-conditioned restaurant. Open for lunch and dinner. Closed on Tuesdays.

Calabas   8285/8485

The Calabas Terrace overlooks the beach at the Divi Flamingo Beach Resort and features an a la carte menu or "all you can eat" buffets. Breakfast is buffet style beginning about 7 A.M., followed by an a la carte lunch and a light afternoon menu. For dinner, special theme nights include Indonesian, barbecue and roast beef. Open daily. Reservations not needed.

At night basket stars expand to feed.
Photo: Dave Brannon.

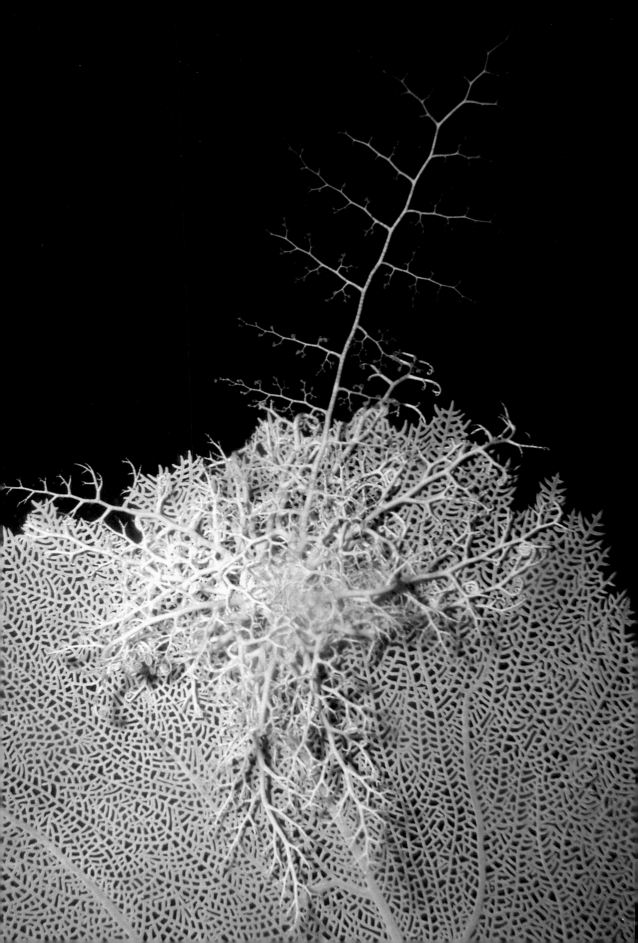

Chibi Chibi   8285/8485

Chibi Chibi is located in a two-story, open air, wooden hamlet overlooking the water at the Divi Flamingo Beach Resort. It is the more expensive and intimate of the two restaurants at the resort. Featured appetizers include a smoked seafood plate and *escargot champignon*. Among the entrees are such dishes as shrimp a la Troy, Antillean bouillabaisse, veal saltimbocca and *keshi yena*, a local chicken dish. The wine list is extensive. International coffees and chocolate mandarin orange cake highlight dessert. Open daily for dinner. Reservations suggested.

Cozzoli's Pizzeria   5195

Cozzoli's is the first pizza parlor on the island, and offers Italian dishes and pizza on an open air terrace overlooking Kralendijk Bay. It is located at the shorefront entrance of the new Harbor Side Shopping Mall. They also offer takeout and delivery service. Open for lunch and dinner. Closed on Sundays.

*A giant anemone (*Condylactis gigantea*) is carving out a home for itself by using the stinging cells in its tentacles to dissolve the living tissue of the coral colony that harbors it. This particular species comes in a variety of colors, including pink-, blue-, green-, and yellow-tipped tentacles. Anemones can move around, by the way. If a location becomes undesirable, an anemone can loosen its grip and slowly creep away, or cut loose entirely and cast its fate to the currents in hopes that it will end up somewhere better. Photo: Larry Martin.*

Green Parrot   5454

The Green Parrot is located next to the dive shop of the Sand Dollar Beach Club and has rapidly established a name for itself as one of the island's leading informal restaurants. The dining area is open air and on the water. Superb service, hearty fare and generous portions are the Green Parrot's trademarks. Another is the flame broiled, fresh caught local fish. If you tire of seafood, the T-bone filet mignon and pasta are also excellent as are the giant hamburgers cooked on the grill.

Mysterious tropical concoctions that are whipped up in the blender are also featured. They all have strange names, some of which are R-rated.

Open for breakfast, lunch and dinner. Reservations not required.

Oasis   8198

Located on Lac Bay, a ten-minute drive from Kralendijk, the Oasis is secluded and intimate. Its imported French wines complement an international cuisine highlighted by many outstanding seafood dishes. Also available are Colombian specialties like *cazuela de mariscos* and p*ez atomatado*. The restaurant's interior is furnished with European antiques. Open for breakfast, lunch and dinner. The bar is open until around midnight. Closed on Mondays. Reservations are not required.

Playa Lechi   5300

The Playa Lechi Restaurant and Bar at the Sunset Beach Hotel offers tropical dining in an attractive open air "beach hut." Steak, lobster, fish and local dishes are found on the menu. Once a week, Indonesian food is featured. The long bar is a great place to watch the sunset or relax listening to local music. The restaurant is open daily. Happy hour is from 5:30 to 7 P.M. Reservations not required.

Kasa Coral   7500

At the Kasa Coral at the Harbour Village Beach Resort, you can start off your day Venezuelan style with either *arepa*, a South American corn bread filled with scrambled eggs, onion, bacon and herbs; or with steak *a caballo*, a beef steak topped with two eggs any style. Lunch entrees include the Bonaire Express, a grilled chicken with Dutch cheese and mango chutney. Dinner choices vary from fresh seafood to rack of lamb. Reservations recommended.

Raffles   8617

Located on Kaya G.E.B. Hellmund near the Divi Flamingo Beach Hotel (look for the red phone booth), Raffles overlooks the harbor from a newly renovated building. Casual and air-conditioned, Raffles specializes in fish and beef dishes prepared French style, and

KLEIN IS ALSO FOR SNORKELERS
As a general rule, the water is somewhat clearer around Klein Bonaire than Bonaire. This is especially true in shallow water, where silty runoff from the land can ruin visibility during rainy periods. Although divers can often get below a dirty surface layer, snorkelers cannot. When visibility is poor on Bonaire, the boat ride out to Klein is usually worth the extra trouble and expense. There are, of course, no guarantees, and Klein can have dirty water too, but even at its worst, it's likely to be better than around Bonaire.

Indonesian food. A specialty is sweet and sour shrimp, and mango parfait. Dinner is served from 6:30 P.M. to midnight. Closed Mondays. Reservations recommended for large groups.

Rendez Vous   8454/8539

This informal and cozy restaurant is located on Kaya L.D. Gerharts in Kralendijk. Unimposing from the outside, the Rendez Vous, owned by Marcel Nahr, is a closely held secret. It lives up to its name, being a favorite meeting place and hangout for many of the dive industry professionals on the island. You might very well run into your dive instructor or dive shop manager here. Photos of the reef and a fascinating montage of the *Hilma Hooker's* sinking decorate the wall.

Homemade soups, fresh fish, seafood, steaks, chops, and a surprisingly extensive selection of vegetarian entrees grace the menu. *Espresso, cappuccino,* and some tasty house specials are

The lighthouse at Punt Vierkant marks the shore entry and exit point. The development adjacent to the lighthouse is private property, so try to maintain a low profile in order to preserve diver access to the site. Photo: Larry Martin.

available. You can eat at the bar or a table in the air-conditioned interior, or be served out on the terrace by the street.

Open for dinner every day except Tuesday. Reservations are recommended.

Rum Runners   8290

Rum Runners Restaurant, located at Captain Don's Habitat, offers casual open air dining on a terrace overlooking the water. If you're in the mood for a hamburger with exotic fixings or a variety of special sandwiches and salads, this is the place to go. Thursday is TexMex night, when Mexican food lovers can sample spicy dishes, and enjoy a mix of country western and local music. Open for breakfast and lunch with dinner served from 7:30 to 11 P.M. Happy hour is Monday through Friday 5 to 7 P.M. and on Saturdays and Sundays from 10 to 11 P.M. Reservations not required.

LOCAL EATING EXPERIENCES

Capricorn

This small local snack bar is located on the seaward side of the main road just south of town. It is within easy walking distance of the Carib Inn or the Flamingo. It doesn't look like a tourist place or even like a restaurant. It has only two tables, and the decor consists of a cable TV tuned to Show Time. The owner, Danny, seems to keep the doors open all the time. He opens up somewhere around 6:30 A.M. for breakfast, stays open through lunch, and if he ever does close, it's well after we went to bed. Besides full sit-down meals, he has ice, beer and other supplies for your cooler.

This is a great place to sample local cooking, particularly for lunch, if you are not in a hurry. Everything is served Bonairean style. Try the fried fish or beer stew or, if you are the adventurous type, try the *kabrito* (goat) stew served with a side of *funchi,* a buttery corn meal mush. Goat is sweeter and more flavorful than beef, but it also tends to have a lot of odd-shaped small bones. Be careful with the homemade hot pickled peppers and onion on the table unless you eat a lot of Mexican food at home.

Lac Snack

This is a place to visit when you are exploring the island. Follow your road map and the signs to Cai, which is at the northeast edge of Lac Bay, the large "bite" in the island's eastern coast. After the long drive on the dirt road through what seems like wilderness, the Lac Snack is the very first sign of civilization you will come to. It is by the water next to the large piles of conch shells.

The food here is basic down-home Bonairean, little changed in centuries. They have fried whole fresh fish, with or without *funchi*, and fried banana, washed down with Amstel.

The main reason to come here is the ambiance; a pleasant shaded terrace, on the edge of the windward reef. The salt-scented breeze comes right off the sea and you can watch the breakers roll in from your table. Too bad they don't have hammocks strung up here to complete the picture. Weekend afternoons, this is a favorite hangout for some of the local fishermen, and it can get a bit noisy at times.

Piles of discarded conch shells line the water at Cai on the northeast edge of Lac Bay.

CONCH RAISING

A traditional island staple is conch (*karko* in Papiamento, or *caracol* in Spanish), a large marine snail with a beautiful pink shell, and tasty, somewhat rubbery flesh. Conch—pronounced "konk"—is eaten as a cocktail snack as well as a main dish. Unfortunately for both the locals and the conchs, there has been an exponential increase in fritter consumption in the last ten years. The conch population around Bonaire and Klein Bonaire has been reduced to a fraction of its former size. Huge shell mounds can be seen around Lac Bay. In an attempt to restore conch numbers, a mariculture lab has been built on the shore of Lac Bay. To visit it, either drive north from Willemstoren Lighthouse, or south from Kralendijk on the road toward Sorobon. You'll see the *Marcultura* laboratory near the turnoff for Sorobon. Call them first at 8595 to be sure they are open for visitors.

CHAPTER IV   DIVING

All the license plates on the cars in Bonaire say "Bonaire: Diver's Paradise," and for good reason. Bonaire's western coast and Klein Bonaire in its lee are protected from the prevailing winds, and offer ideal diving conditions almost 365 days a year. Warm, calm and clear water with gentle currents are the norm in Bonaire.

The island's beautiful coral reefs, teeming with tropical, fishes, have made Bonaire one of the world's premiere dive destinations.

UNDERWATER TOPOGRAPHY

It has been said that there are only two dive sites here: Bonaire and Klein Bonaire. Although this overstates the case, it is true that the majority of dive sites on both islands have fairly similar underwater topography, and similar kinds of animals at equivalent depths. Of course, there are many small-scale differences among sites, and a few sites have quite unusual terrain.

Shelves. Nearly every site has a shallow, relatively flat underwater shelf or terrace 10–30 feet (3–9 m) deep next to the shoreline. The terrace gradually slopes upward to the beach in most locations, but some sites with ironshore cliffs, such as those to the north on Bonaire, have a terrace that ends abruptly at the base of a cliff.

The shelf surface is usually a gritty, hard substrate of consolidated calcium carbonate, made up of limestone bits, sand, dead coral, calcareous algae, gorgonian spicules and other carbonaceous material that has become cemented together by natural processes.

Depressions in the shelf often fill with loose sand, especially near sandy beaches or other sources of sediment. Corals, gorgonians and other sessile animals on the shelf sometimes look as if they are growing on sand, but they originally settled on an exposed hard surface. Beneath the sand, they are still attached to that firm substrate.

Prominent corals on the shelf include fire coral, staghorn coral and elkhorn coral. Huge gorgonians are abundant in many locations. Abundant fishes on the shelf include parrotfishes, peacock flounders, sand divers and other lizardfishes, tobaccofish, harlequin basslets, bar jacks, blue tang, great barracudas, damselfishes, creole wrasses, creole-fish, mojarras, goatfishes, trunkfishes, cowfishes, puffers and porcupinefishes, sand tilefish, and snappers. Occasionally, snook, mullet and bonefish are seen in sandy areas. Most of the conchs that used to roam the shelf have been turned into conch fritters, but a number of less palatable large snails are often seen on the sand.

Slopes. Seaward of the shelf, nearly all sites have gentle, coral- and sponge-covered slopes that begin with a low ridge, and end more or less abruptly in sand flats at their bases. A few locations, especially on the south side of Klein, near Karpata, and at Boca Bartól, have long spurs or buttresses with sand channels between them, rather than wide slopes. Other spots such as Carl's Hill, Cliff, and Rappel have short vertical walls or distinctive steps or terraces, rather than a single unbroken slope.

Toward the upper parts of the slope, important corals include mountainous and cavernous star corals, brain and starlet corals,

The flamingo tongue is a snail that eats gorgonian tissues, which then exposes the stalks to settling sponges and other invaders. The flamingo tongue's spotted mantle can be completely retracted, revealing a pearly pink shell. Photo: George Lewbel.

flower corals, yellow pencil corals, club finger corals, and in a few places, pillar corals. The lower slopes are dominated by species that specialize in lower-light environments, such as plate or sheet corals. At the bases of slopes, huge stacks of sheet corals dominate the scene. Common fishes on the slopes include grunts, squirrelfishes, yellowtail snappers, angelfishes (especially queen angelfish), rock and red hinds, coneys, graysbys, Nassau groupers, hamlets, fairy and blackcap basslets, morays, spotted drums, blue and brown chromis, Spanish hogfish and butterflyfishes.

Sand Flats. On Bonaire, most of the drop-offs hit the sand in the range of 110 to 130 feet (34 to 40 m), but it is possible to get much deeper in many locations. On Klein, where the water tends to be clearer, coral growth extends downward in excess of 150 feet (46 m) at several sites. Deep sand flats have their own inhabitants, such as beds of garden eels, porgies, southern stingrays, large hermit crabs and sand tilefish. Here, too, conchs can get away from most of their predators, and are sometimes seen feeding on low-lying algae. At depths of 150 feet (46 m) or more, huge barrel sponges and beds of deep-water gorgonians crop up where hard substrate is exposed or thinly covered by sand.

Dive Site Identification

Shortly after the Bonaire Marine Park was established in 1979, 44 sites were included in the *Guide to the Bonaire Marine Park*. Fixed moorings were installed at most of these sites. All sites were given official park numbers, beginning with the lowest numbers toward the south, and the highest toward the north.

Although the reefs and their access points are more or less the same at the old park sites these days, the numbering system is no longer that simple. Additional moorings have been emplaced between the original moorings. New moorings have been named and given numbers by the dive operators who installed them, but in some cases, operators have reassigned old site numbers to new sites. A letter system has been instituted for new sites that lie between old sites (e.g., 4A, 4B, 4C between buoys 4 and 5).

To avoid confusion, we've skipped the numbering system almost entirely, and have relied on site names. There are several reasons for this. First, the numbering scheme is likely to be changed substantially in the future. More sites are being added to keep up with increased diver traffic, and nobody wants to log in a great dive site as "Bonaire Number 94F." Second, the island dive guides know the sites primarily by name and location, rather than by buoy number.

We have provided numbers for the old park sites along the Bonaire coast to facilitate shore diving at those locations where marker stones may still be present.

Some sites—especially the older ones—have several names in common use. For consistency, we have stuck with the names in the *Guide to the Bonaire Marine Park* whenever possible, though sites established since 1983 don't appear in the Park guide. We've picked the name that seemed most appropriate to us, with all due respect to anyone who prefers one of the alternative names which we have also included.

A few of the older park sites are no longer in good condition, although they are still dived. We have used our own judgment in omitting these damaged sites, leaving in only those places that we would pay good money to dive!

Water Temperature and Visibility

The water temperature in Bonaire ranges from 78 to 86°F (26 to 30°C). About three years out of every five, upwellings of cold, nutrient rich bottom water from the deep Atlantic spill into the Caribbean over the relatively shallow shelf that connects Trinidad with the Grenadines to the east of Bonaire. This water then circulates westward. When this happens—usually during July—water temperatures can drop to about 72°F (22°C) and visibility can fall to 30 feet (9 m) or less in all areas. These conditions can last anywhere from one or two days up to a week or more.

Sometimes this cold upwelling water does not come all the way to the surface but is only encountered at depth as a murky thermocline. Though diving during these periods is not as comfortable as it could be, it is still a lot nicer than the local quarry, and the reef seems to benefit. It could just be imagination, but the colors of the corals and other organisms seem brighter during and immediately after one of these upwellings.

During most other times, visibility averages between 60-90 feet (18-27 m) near the hotels on the central west coast to 90-120 feet (27-36 m) on Klein Bonaire well away from the most populated areas.

DEPTHS

For each site, the depth range for the best coral, sponge growth or other main attractions is given. Depths are also given for individual features, such as the edge of the shallow shelf found at most sites.

The depths, which are given in both feet and meters (rounded off to the nearest foot or meter) are approximate. They may not match your own gauge for three important reasons: 1) gauges vary in accuracy, 2) sites change over time, and 3) your location may differ from the place where we took our depth readings. It is critical, therefore, to monitor your instruments during the course of a dive.

The greatest depth given for each site does not indicate the maximum depth of the site. It refers only to the greatest depth where there are features of interest, and it is not a recommendation to go that deep. Divers' abilities vary greatly. What constitutes a safe depth for an experienced diver may be extremely hazardous for a novice.

At nearly every site, it is easy to exceed most training agencies' recommended scuba limits of 130 feet (40 m) by proceeding just a short distance farther offshore. Depths of some topographic features beyond the sport diving range are given for navigational purposes only. For instance, the sand flats at the base of many slopes on Klein Bonaire begin in the 150- to 160-foot (46-49 m) range. In many cases, depths greater than 130 feet (40 m) were determined by reading diver-held sonar instruments, looking down from shallower water.

Since coral-covered slopes seem steep by comparison to the sand bottom at their bases, you may get the mistaken impression that the sand bottom is level. It is not. As you leave the reef, the sand in most places gets deeper and

deeper, and there are few visual cues to alert you to the increasing depth. Any time you're on the sand at the base of the drop-off, there's an excellent chance that you've exceeded 100 feet (30 m). The farther from the coral you are, the deeper you are, as a general rule.

MOORINGS

To prevent damage to reefs, boats are not allowed to anchor within the Bonaire Marine Park. Boats must use fixed moorings. These moorings consist of buoys attached by lines to large concrete-filled drums, cement blocks, or other semi-permanent objects on the bottom. The mooring anchors were placed in shallow water near the shelf crests, adjacent to drop-offs. The easiest way to keep your bearings at most marked sites is to descend on the mooring line, note the depth of the anchor, and then proceed down-slope and upcurrent. At the end of a dive, head back up-slope to the depth of the anchor, swim along until you see it, and make your safety stop near the anchor or on the line.

Conveniently, most anchors are at an appropriate depth for a safety stop. Keep in mind that 1) nothing is permanent in the ocean, 2) mooring lines occasionally break, 3) mooring anchors can shift in locations and depths, and 4) buoys are frequently not where you expect them to be.

SHORE MARKERS

Many of the old sites along the road on Bonaire were originally marked with large stones painted yellow that bore the official Park numbers. After falling into some disrepair the marker system has been revived and is now maintained by the Bonaire Marine Park staff. We've given site numbers for the older Park sites on Bonaire (where stones were originally present) to help you find them. If you plan on shore diving, ask your divemaster for a current list of stone numbers and marked sites.

Reefs vs. Divers

Although buoys and shoreline markers may give the impression that they are "real" sites, the reef away from these markers is in better condition than at the markers themselves. The reason is, simply, the heavy diver traffic at the marked sites. Hundreds of thousands of dives have been made at the older sites, and some of them are showing signs of wear despite increased emphasis on buoyancy control.

Bonaire's larger dive operators have agreed informally to limit their use of the more popular dive sites in order to prevent them from deteriorating further. Also, the Bonaire Marine Park authorities periodically declare damaged sites off limits to allow them to recover. In fact, the entire area between Karpata and Goto Meer (a flamingo sanctuary) is permanently closed. You can do your part for reef conservation by supporting this policy. Don't put your dive guide in a bind by insisting on going to a site which is temporarily out of service.

No Gloves. For years, divers wore gloves to protect their hands from reefs, which were viewed by most people as sharp, inert objects, not much more alive than rocks are. We now know better, and in an effort to protect living reefs from hands, wearing gloves is prohibited in the Marine Park.

Coral is fragile and easily damaged by abrasion. The outer surface of a healthy coral head is covered with a thin film of living tissue. When intact, this tissue protects the underlying calcium carbonate skeleton that most of us think of as "coral." Tissue that is scraped by gloved hands (or fins, knee pads, etc.) may die, exposing the skeleton to attack by parasites and algae. A small damaged spot may result in the death of the entire coral head. By banning gloves, divers are encouraged to look, not touch. For shore entries, gloves can be worn and then removed once in the water.

Park Rules. Virtually all of the diveable sites on Bonaire and Klein Bonaire are within the Bonaire Marine Park, which covers coral reefs from the high tide watermark down to a depth of 200 feet (60 m). Park rules prohibit diving in closed areas (ask your dive operator where they are); spearfishing; harassing, damaging, or collecting any living or dead marine organisms, including shells; prying up attached or embedded nautical artifacts; anchoring most vessels; and littering. The rules for visiting divers boil down to three basic good diving techniques: 1) look but don't touch, 2) take nothing but pictures, and 3) leave nothing but bubbles.

The Bonaire Marine Park charges all divers, snorkellers and others using the Park an admission fee of $10 per year. The fees are the only regular income of the Park.

Boat Diving

Most dive sites on Bonaire are accessible both by boat and from shore. However, not all dive operators run boats to all locations. The more distant sites require longer travel times. Sites south of Punt Vierkant or north of Thousand Steps sometimes have choppy surface conditions, which can make for a rocky boat ride. Second, anchoring within the Park is not permitted except at a fixed mooring, and no moorings are found at some sites.

Shore Diving

In this era of fast, comfortable boats most divers don't realize that nearly all Bonaire diving was once done from shore. There are many excellent sites where there are still no moorings and the reef is beautiful and almost untouched.

Car rentals are readily available and even the sites on the south and north of the island are just a short drive away. In addition, some operators run "expeditions" to various shore points and provide truck transportation for divers and their gear.

If diving in front of a hotel where you are not a guest, be sure to ask permission first.

With the exception of Lighthouse, Red Slave, La Dania's Leap, Playa Bengé and Boca Bartól, most shore sites have relatively easy entry and exit points under calm conditions. Rough conditions, however, can render any entry or exit hazardous, and beach topography can change over time. An experienced diver may be able to handle surf that is dangerous to a novice, but only if trained in surf entires and exits. Our rule of thumb: "If in doubt, sit it out!"

For your protection, we recommend that you wear gloves, boots and wet suits for all shore dive entries and exits except those off sandy beaches and docks in front of hotels.

Bonaire's ironshore is completely unforgiving of errors in judgment or balance. On the reef, you can put your gloves in your BC pocket, but you'll be glad to have them along when it comes time to make your way back to the beach.

SNORKELING

Many sites have broad shelves covered with coral or other features of interest. These places are best for snorkelers, and are labeled with an (S). Sites without an (S) have shelves that are too sandy, deep or narrow to offer much to snorkelers, even though they are often excellent places for divers to make a safety stop.

In almost all cases snorkelers are welcome on dive boats and there are many fine snorkeling sites on Klein Bonaire that are only accessible by boat.

WINDWARD DIVING

Sites on the windward coast of Bonaire are not included in this book because they are exposed to heavy weather most of the time, and are therefore rarely diveable. Some operators do run boat trips to the windward side when the weather is bad on the leeward side, or when conditions are exceptionally calm. It is, however, a long haul—over 20 miles (32 k) from Kralendijk.

The windward side is seldom calm enough to dive from the beach. Even when local conditions appear placid, ocean swells generated far away by the trade winds can crash unexpectedly onto the shore. The energy released when a swell suddenly encounters land should never be underestimated.

During those brief periods of calm, the huge sponges, gorgonians, coral, and the prolific fish life found on the windward side are well worth the trip.

REQUIRED SKILL LEVELS

Except where indicated in the site description, all the dive sites are suitable for any well-trained, certified sport diver in good physical shape when water conditions are calm. Due to the gentle underwater topography of most

Excellent snorkeling can be found on most of the shallow shelves ringing Bonaire and Klein Bonaire. Photo: Keith Ibsen.

ETIQUETTE FOR VISITING DIVERS

If you're diving in front of your own hotel, chances are that you'll be briefed by the dive operator on their procedures and the entry and exit locations. However, a little extra courtesy is appropriate if you intend to dive from a beach or a dock in front of a hotel where you're not a guest. Hotel staff members have to deal with noise and litter from their own guests, and they can be very sensitive about outsiders who may increase their work load. Furthermore, when you dive in front of a hotel without patronizing its dive operator, you're doing the equivalent of bringing a bag lunch into a restaurant. Before you use a hotel's facilities, take a moment to ask how they prefer to handle visiting divers. Chances are excellent that you'll be welcomed, and treated with more respect than if you just barge in.

Tiny decorator crabs—sometimes called sponge crabs—are probably unpalatable to fishes because of the living sponges they attach to their backs. The sponges also act as camouflage during the daytime, when decorator crabs are usually hidden in crevices. This photo was taken at night, when decorator crabs are out foraging. Photo: George Lewbel.

sites and lack of waves or strong currents, novices can simply stay shallow, while more experienced divers can go deeper if desired. At most sites, currents are imperceptible or mild.

The exceptions are Lighthouse, Red Slave, Playa Bengé, and Boca Bartól, which usually have rough water and strong currents. Most of the time, they cannot be dived safely from the beach. Even when water conditions appear to be perfect, very strong currents and unpredictable surf may be encountered. Consequently, these sites should be attempted from the beach only by advanced divers in good physical condition with considerable experience in rough water entries and exits.

Divers going off the beach at these sites should always leave someone observant on shore who can assist with a difficult exit, or go for help if necessary. It's a good idea for all beach dives, but a must for these sites.

EQUIPMENT

Well maintained rental equipment is available through all the major dive operations. When bringing your own gear, however, you should also bring backups if you have them. It might save you a frustrating trip hunting all over the island for a replacement part such as a hose or low pressure BC connector. If you are comfortable renting unfamiliar gear then leave the spares at home.

WARNING: BOAT TRAFFIC

Bonaire and Klein Bonaire sometimes have heavy boat traffic, especially near dive sites. Moorings at more popular sites may be in use by dive boats throughout the day, while other sites such as the Town Pier sometimes have vessels coming and going even at night. Be especially alert when in the vicinity of any recognized dive site, whether you're diving from a boat or from the shore.

In addition, there are many sailboats in the area, and they don't make much noise while underway. Keep your eyes open when on or near the surface!

The shore near Boca Onimá is usually pounded by heavy waves. Stay away from the edges of the cliffs on the windward side of the island even if conditions appear calm since occasional large breakers can be dangerous. Photo: Dave Brannon.

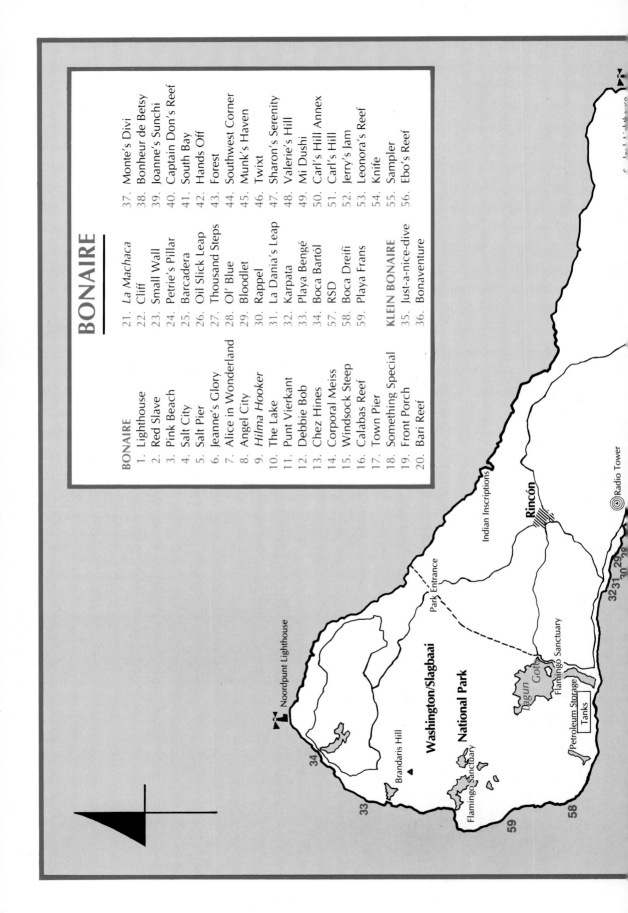

BONAIRE

BONAIRE
1. Lighthouse
2. Red Slave
3. Pink Beach
4. Salt City
5. Salt Pier
6. Jeanne's Glory
7. Alice in Wonderland
8. Angel City
9. *Hilma Hooker*
10. The Lake
11. Punt Vierkant
12. Debbie Bob
13. Chez Hines
14. Corporal Meiss
15. Windsock Steep
16. Calabas Reef
17. Town Pier
18. Something Special
19. Front Porch
20. Bari Reef

21. *La Machaca*
22. Cliff
23. Small Wall
24. Petrie's Pillar
25. Barcadera
26. Oil Slick Leap
27. Thousand Steps
28. Ol' Blue
29. Bloodlet
30. Rappel
31. La Dania's Leap
32. Karpata
33. Playa Bengé
34. Boca Bartól
57. RSD
58. Boca Dreifi
59. Playa Frans

KLEIN BONAIRE
35. Just-a-nice-dive
36. Bonaventure

37. Monte's Divi
38. Bonheur de Betsy
39. Joanne's Sunchi
40. Captain Don's Reef
41. South Bay
42. Hands Off
43. Forest
44. Southwest Corner
45. Munk's Haven
46. Twixt
47. Sharon's Serenity
48. Valerie's Hill
49. Mi Dushi
50. Carl's Hill Annex
51. Carl's Hill
52. Jerry's Jam
53. Leonora's Reef
54. Knife
55. Sampler
56. Ebo's Reef

Noordpunt Lighthouse

Washington/Slagbaai
National Park

Brandaris Hill

Flamingo Sanctuary

Park Entrance

Indian Inscriptions

Rincón

Radio Tower

Tagun Gotbo

Flamingo Sanctuary

Petroleum Storage
Tanks

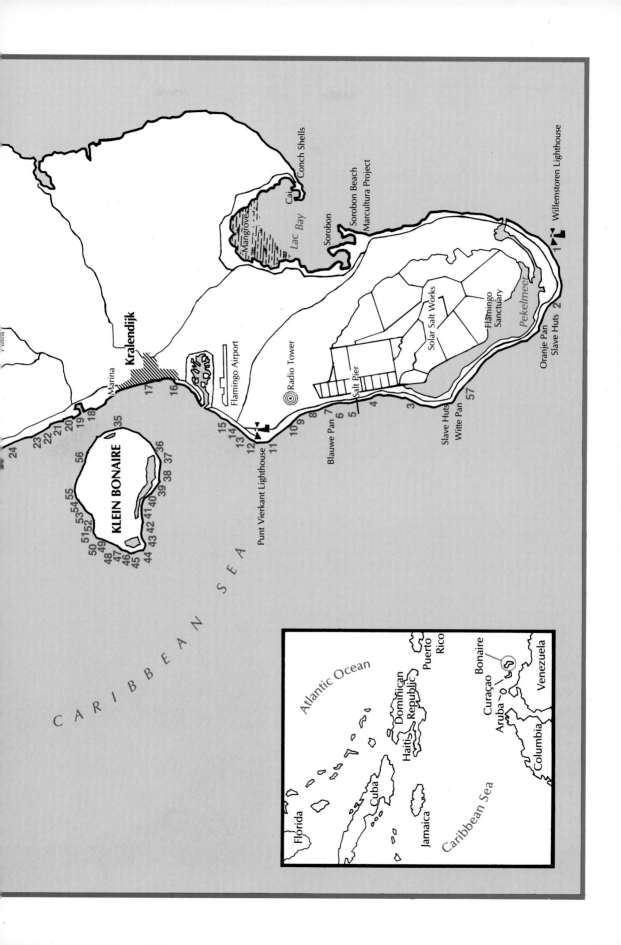

Conch Shells

Cai

Lac Bay

Mangrove

Sorobon Beach

Sorobon

Marcultura Project

Willemstoren Lighthouse

1

2

Slave Huts

Oranje Pan

Pekelmeer

Flamingo
Sanctuary

Solar Salt Works

57

3

Witte Pan

Slave Huts

4

5

6

7

Blauwe Pan

8

9

10

Salt Pier

Radio Tower

Flamingo Airport

Kralendijk

Marina

17

16

15

14

13

12

11

Punt Vierkant Lighthouse

18

19

20

21

22

23

24

KLEIN BONAIRE

35

56

36

37

38

39

40

41

42

43

44

45

46

47

48

49

50

51

52

53

54

55

C A R I B B E A N   S E A

Atlantic Ocean

Florida

Cuba

Jamaica

Haiti

Dominican
Republic

Puerto
Rico

Bonaire

Curaçao

Aruba

Venezuela

Columbia

Caribbean Sea

CHAPTER **V**   **DIVE SITES**

LEEWARD BONAIRE

1. LIGHTHOUSE

DEPTH:	30-60 FEET (9-18 M)
LEVEL:	VERY EXPERIENCED
ACCESS:	SHORE
PARK SITE:	1

Because of the surf and currents usually present here, only very experienced divers in good condition should dive this site. It has excellent gorgonians and elkhorn coral, as well as a scattering of wreck debris. This site is sometimes referred to as Willemstoren.

Directions. There is no buoy at Lighthouse, but it is impossible to miss. Drive down the coastal road south of Kralendijk (don't take the cutoff for Lac Bay), continue past Punt Vierkant, the Trans World Radio Antennas, the Salt Pier and the two sets of slave huts. You will soon come to a massive lighthouse marking the southern end of Bonaire.

The Dive. The easiest entry and exit may be found just west of the lighthouse, although beach contours change so the best spot may differ from visit to visit. The shoreline is a cobble beach, and heavy surf usually makes the area unsafe for beach access. However, if you catch it during a calm period, you'll have a spectacular dive. During entry watch out for the boulders in the shallow water, and be sure to protect your mask and regulator. Ducking under waves may be hazardous. The current comes up from the south, and splits near the lighthouse to go along the windward and leeward coasts of Bonaire. Eddies and current reversals are common, though the

usual current direction at Lighthouse is from west to east.

Once beyond the surf zone, begin your descent while swimming against the current. On most days, that will be to the right, facing the sea from the beach. If the current is running from the opposite direction, turn left as you face the sea to begin your dive. If you are unable to make reasonable headway against the current, or if current direction changes during your dive, abort the dive and return to the beach. At the end of your dive, you should be able to ride with the current back to your exit point.

Fish at Lighthouse tend to be skittish, since they don't often have terrestrial visitors. Large pelagic species such as jacks are often seen. There is a large gorgonian bed on the shallow shelf, and some excellent elkhorn coral heads are also there. Another attraction is the assortment of old anchors, chains and other wreck debris. Many ships came to grief near Willemstoren before the lighthouse was installed in 1838.

The upper portion of the slope has outstanding corals and sponges, but the lower portions are not as lush. Most divers will enjoy the shallower areas more than the deeper areas of this dive. The slope hits sand bottom at about 130 feet (40 m).

Christmas tree worms highlight a mosaic of at least 25 invertebrate species in an area the size of a hand. Photo: George Lewbel.

Willemstoren Lighthouse marks the southern end of Bonaire. The keeper's house is in disrepair and the light is automated, but the lighthouse continues to serve mariners, as it has for over 150 years. Photo: George Lewbel.

2. RED SLAVE

DEPTH:	30-90 FEET (9-27 M)
LEVEL:	EXPERIENCED
ACCESS:	SHORE
PARK SITE:	2

The main attraction of this site is the scattered remains of the *HMS Barham* now mostly covered with coral. Red Slave is also known as Rode Pan, Pietiké or Peliké.

Directions. Take the coastal road south from Kralendijk as in the directions given for Lighthouse until you come to the second set of slave huts.

The Dive. The easiest entry and exit is immediately adjacent to the slave huts. The shoreline at Red Slave is similar to that at Lighthouse. The beach is covered with cobbles and coral rubble, and is occasionally exposed to heavy surf, though it is a more protected site than Lighthouse. As such, it sometimes makes a good fallback in case Lighthouse is marginally diveable.

Caution. Strong, unpredictable currents are typical at Red Slave. The average water movement is from south to north, meaning that most dives should begin with a left turn (facing the sea from the beach) into the current.

From a reef standpoint, Red Slave is rather barren, having a series of ridges and sand-filled valleys. There are many large gorgonians and sponges, and quite a few pelagic fishes and groupers have been reported at the site. However, the main attraction is the wreck of the *HMS Barham*, a British warship that ran aground here in 1829 and was destroyed by the surf. Ballast stones, anchors and cannons have been recovered. By now, most of the remains of the wreck have been covered with coral growth or buried in sand, but you might get lucky. If you do find any archaeological artifacts, take nothing but pictures. The site is legally protected.

3. PINK BEACH (S)

DEPTH:	30-90 FEET (9-27 M)
ACCESS:	SHORE
PARK SITE:	3

Pink Beach, also known as Witte Pan or Cabajé, is popular with locals, and a very good choice for a low-stress, low-strain beach dive.

Directions. Pink Beach is south of Kralendijk, just past the evaporating ponds of the salt works. After you pass the Salt Pier, keep your eye out for a large, white abandoned building adjacent to a set of slave huts on the ocean side of the road. Park off the road to the right. The pinkish sand beach is to the north of the large building.

The Dive. The surf is usually calm here, offering an easy entry and exit. Typically, the current is mild. The mooring is at a depth of about 15 feet (5 m) on a broad, sandy shelf, but the buoy is often missing due to wave action. Gorgonian beds are found in some areas of the shelf. Seaward of the mooring, a staghorn coral bed merges into a coral-covered slope at about 30 feet (9 m). Corals and sponges on the slope are in very good condition, perhaps due to the relative lack of diver traffic. Fish life is prolific, and you're likely to see some uncommon species that shun more popular dive sites. The slope ends on a sand bottom at around 90–100 feet (27–30 m). The sand is a good place to spot peacock flounders, lizardfishes, yellow-headed jawfish, and other fishes that prefer a sandy bottom.

4. SALT CITY (S)

DEPTH:	INNER REEF 30-70 FEET (9-21 M)
	OUTER REEF 70-125 FEET (21-38 M)
ACCESS:	BOAT OR SHORE
PARK SITE:	4

Sometimes referred to as The Invisibles or Saliña Abou, this site is the southernmost one in the Alice in Wonderland double-reef complex.

Directions. It may be reached either by boat, or from the road south of Kralendijk. The buoy for Salt City is about 600 feet (182 m) south of the Salt Pier.

OBELISKS

The name Red Slave is derived from the red obelisk near the slave huts. This obelisk was one of four navigational markers used by inbound ships. As they approached the island, they were signaled to anchor near one of the markers to pick up their cargoes of salt. The four obelisks were colored to match the Dutch flag: red (*rode*), white (*witte*), blue (*blauwe*), and orange (*oranje*). Each denoted a separate salt "pan" or evaporating pond. The orange obelisk is gone now, but the others remain. The white obelisk is near Pink Beach, the blue obelisk is near the Salt Pier, and the red obelisk is near Red Slave.

The Dive. The beach here is sandy with coral rubble. You can enter adjacent to the buoy, which is in about 30 feet (9 m) of water just a few minutes' swim offshore. There is, however, an easier entry and exit 1500 feet (450 m) farther south. A wide sand channel visible from the beach can be followed all the way to the base of the first slope.

Excellent Snorkeling. The shelf at Salt City is quite broad and excellent for snorkeling. There is a wide variety of shallow-water coral, including quite a bit of elkhorn and staghorn coral, and lots of gorgonians. The shelf seaward of the buoy turns downward sharply at about 30 feet (9 m), and the slope of this first reef drops to a sand flat about 75 feet (23 m) deep. The slope to the sand flat has many gorgonians on it, though its coral cover is poor.

If you're comfortable with greater depths, we recommend proceeding beyond this inner reef to the outer reef. On your way, slow down and have a look around the sand flat between the two reefs. Stay alert and you'll find an extensive colony of garden eels and a number of large sand tilefish nests.

On the outer edge of the sand flat, the low-lying second reef rises up to about 70 feet (21 m) from the surface. This reef is not as pronounced as at the other Alice in Wonderland sites such as Angel City. It consists of several narrow, discontinuous ridges or coral islands with sand patches in between. It's a great place to see fish that don't often come near shore. Pelagic species such as jacks are frequently seen over the outer reef.

The outer reef slopes off gradually on its outer edge, dropping gently but steadily into deeper water. There are some enormous vase sponges on this outer slope, in about 125 feet (38 m) of water.

5. SALT PIER

DEPTH:	40-70 FEET (12-21 M)
ACCESS:	BOAT OR SHORE

The Salt Pier makes a great afternoon dive when the sun filters through the pilings producing wonderful shadows and silhouettes.

Directions. The Salt Pier is located at the salt works of the Antilles International Salt Company, a few minutes' drive south of the airport. You'll know it when you see it. It's a huge structure crossing the road, supporting a conveyer belt from the salt mounds. Its function is to transfer salt from these mounds to freighters docked at the pier. Consequently, it should never be dived when there are any vessels operating in the vicinity or tied to the pier. If in doubt, ask at the salt company office, up the clearly-marked driveway across the road from the pier.

In the afternoon the sun silhouettes divers between the pilings of the Salt Pier and throws flickering beams of light on the bottom. Tarpon are often seen beneath the outer part of the Pier. Photo: Larry Martin.

Sea salt is dried in mounds after washing and then loaded on ships by conveyor belts which lead out to the end of the Salt Pier.

The blue obelisk near the Salt Pier served as a navigational aid to incoming salt ships in earlier days. The Pier is an outstanding afternoon dive when no vessel traffic is in the vicinity. Photo: Larry Martin.

SOLAR SALT PANS

In the southern part of Bonaire are the vast salt works that have been an important part of the economy since the 1600's. Sea water flows into the Pekelmeer or salt lake by wave and tidal action. It is then pumped into condenser and saturation ponds. When the ponds are almost fully saturated with salt brine, the solution is moved to crystallizers where the water evaporates, leaving only the salt.

After harvesting, the salt is washed and stacked into long rows where it drains and dries for several months. You can see these huge mounds of salt opposite the Salt Pier on the main road south of town. The conveyor belt extending onto the Salt Pier can load 2,000 tons an hour onto ships. Most of Bonaire's salt is exported to the eastern United States, New Zealand, and other areas of the Caribbean. It is used primarily for industrial applications, water softening, and ice control.

The Dive. Dive boats often tie up to the buoy near the pier, but it can be dived from shore very easily. To dive from shore, park near the base of the pier and either climb over the concrete blocks, or wade in at the little cobble beach just to the right of the pier. You can exit at the same location. Be careful, and skip the shore dive if there's any surf running. There are plenty of small rocks just beneath the surface in water less than 3 feet (1 m) deep, and you'll bang up your shins and drop your camera if you try it when the water's rough. Under the pier, watch out for cables, fishing line and sharp metal junk.

The Salt Pier invites comparison with the Town Pier, one of the best-known and best-loved dive sites in the Caribbean. The Salt Pier has some orange cup corals, but not nearly as many as the Town Pier, and the pilings are less overgrown since the Salt Pier is a newer structure. As a night dive, it runs a second to the Town Pier, though there is less monofilament under the Salt Pier and it's almost never crowded.

The large purple "linguini" sponge at Jeanne's Glory. Photo: Larry Martin.

The fish aren't particularly tame at the Salt Pier because they haven't seen all that many divers. Schools of blue tang swirl around the pier, and there are large tube sponges projecting outward from the pilings.

Photo Tip. Photographers will want to set up for wide angle so they can shoot pilings and divers.

6. JEANNE'S GLORY (S)

DEPTH:	30-110 FEET (9-34 M)
ACCESS:	BOAT OR SHORE

Larger sponges, including barrel sponges, are one of the main features of this site.

Directions. Jeanne's Glory is the first site north of the Salt Pier. Its small buoy is moored just north of a very large metal can-like buoy on the northern side of the Salt Pier.

The Dive. If you're diving from the beach, you can get in and out at the same place suggested for the Salt Pier, but you'll have a fairly long swim to Jeanne's Glory. It's easier to pick an access spot along the rocky shore in a line with the small buoy. Be careful of rough terrain in shallow water, and don't attempt a shore dive if there are any waves. Also, be watchful of the large anchor chain between the two buoys. It is covered with fire coral.

The shelf at Jeanne's Glory has large gorgonians and a very active fish community. The slope begins at around 30 feet (9 m) and continues downward to sand at about 110 feet (34 m). There is a huge, nest-like purple "linguini" or finger sponge seaward of the buoy at 45 feet (14 m), and very dense coral and sponge cover all the way down the slope. Another very interesting feature of the site is a group of small barrel sponges on the sand at 110 feet (34 m). If you've dived elsewhere in the Caribbean, you may have noticed how few barrel sponges there seem to be around Bonaire. There actually are quite a few of them, especially off Klein Bonaire, but they're mostly very deep.

7. ALICE IN WONDERLAND (S)

DEPTH:	INNER REEF 30-90 FEET (9-27 M)
	OUTER REEF 70-120 FEET (21-36 M)
ACCESS:	BOAT OR SHORE
PARK SITE:	5

Alice in Wonderland is a large, continuous double-reef complex running parallel to the shore.

Directions. This site can be found by driving south of Kralendijk on the coast road, past the Trans World Radio antennas, and stopping just north of the Salt Pier to count the buoys. The big buoy north of the Salt Pier is a very large mooring for ships. There are four smaller buoys further north, all within sight of each other. The first small buoy marks Jeanne's Glory and the second small buoy, which is moored in about 15 feet (5 m) of water, marks Alice in Wonderland.

The Dive. Directly offshore, there is a shallow shelf covered with large gorgonian sea fans, staghorn coral and fire coral. Many parrotfish and lizardfish can usually be seen there. The inner reef begins seaward of the shelf at about 30 feet (9 m). It is a coral and sponge-covered wall, sloping downward to a broad, white sand channel at about 90 feet (27 m). The sand channel is over 100 feet (30 m) wide, and has a colony of garden eels. Tiger groupers are often seen along the edges of the channel. At night, orange ball anemones expand at the bases of coral heads just above the sand.

Good Deep Dive. If you're interested in a deep dive, the outer reef, which is much more spectacular than the inner reef, is a very good choice. On the seaward (west) side of the sand channel, there is a coral-covered ridge, rising 20 feet (6 m) out of the sand to a depth of about 70 feet (21 m) at its shallowest. This outer reef has some very large brain corals, and is an excellent place to see larger fishes such as horse-eye jacks, big groupers, and log-sized barracudas. Queen triggerfish are often sighted there, too.

The seaward side of the ridge slopes off into the blue, with most of the coral cover ending at about 120 feet (36 m). If you're trying to conserve air or time for a multi-level dive, it makes sense to stay as shallow as possible for the traverse from the inner reef across the sand channel to the outer reef. Be certain to keep the bottom in view, and return toward the shoreline if you lose sight of the bottom. Past the second reef, there's nothing but the abyss beneath you.

8. ANGEL CITY (S)

DEPTH:	30-70 FEET (9-21 M)
ACCESS:	BOAT OR SHORE
PARK SITE:	6

Just like Alice in Wonderland, Angel City consists of a double-reef system: a slope separated from a ridge by a sand channel, all parallel to shore.

Directions. Access from shore is from the coast road south of Kralendijk and north of the salt works. Entry is directly opposite the Trans World Radio towers. The site is marked by the third small buoy to the north of the pier.

The Dive. The buoy is only a few hundred feet from shore, moored in about 20 feet (6 m) of water on a shallow, gorgonian-covered shelf with lots of staghorn and fire coral. The shelf merges smoothly into a slope that drops gently down onto a sand channel around 60–70 feet (18–21 m) deep. The sand channel is much narrower than at Alice in Wonderland. You'll be able to see the outer reef from the inner side of the sand channel. The sand channel is crossed by "bridges" of broken coral.

Large Purple Tube Sponge. At this point, we suggest that you turn right (north) and stay over the sand for a short distance. You'll soon come to one of the largest purple tube sponges on Bonaire, standing guard over one of the bridges across the sand at a depth of about 70 feet (21 m). Enroute you are likely to see tiger groupers.

After viewing the sponge, swim back southward along the crest of the outer reef. On your right will be a drop-off ending in very deep water, but most of the fish at this site tend to stay in shallower water. The outer reef drop-off here is not as spectacular as at other sites close by, so we suggest not dropping over the edge down the outer slope. Horse-eye jacks often feed above the outer reef.

The outer reef rises to a depth of about 30 feet (9 m) at the southern end of the sand channel. You'll find a group of tall, eroded coral heads that are usually surrounded by large, schooling black margates, along with schoolmaster snappers. Continue shoreward, back up the inner reef slope and northward to return to the buoy. On your way, keep your eye out for a huge, castle-like mountainous star coral head at 25 feet (8 m) with a small cave on one side, and portrait-sized holes in the other.

9. HILMA HOOKER

DEPTH:	65-95 FEET (20-29 M)
SUNK:	1984
TYPE:	FREIGHTER
LENGTH:	236 FEET (72 M)
ACCESS:	BOAT OR SHORE

History. The *Hilma Hooker* is a freighter that sank in 1984 following a search and drug bust by the local authorities. Stories differ about why she began to take on water. Some say that the search that uncovered the secret compartments filled with marijuana also "accidentally" opened some holes in her hull. Others say she was in poor repair, and when she was seized, the owners (for obvious reasons) didn't come forward. In any event, when everyone knew that she was sinking, the authorities towed her out and let her down gently onto a sand bottom at the base of a wall.

Directions. The site is just seaward of the antennas for Trans World Radio, near the Alice in Wonderland complex between Punt Vierkant and the Salt Pier. There are several moorings close together over the site, spanning the distance between the wreck's bow and stern. The moorings are visible from the coastal road. If you're diving from the beach, swim out to whichever mooring is free to avoid the boat crowds. There's usually a boat at one or more moorings as it's a very popular site. It is the only site on Bonaire where more than one dive boat is allowed to tie up simultaneously.

The Dive. The easiest way to dive the *Hooker* is to descend on the buoy line, explore the upper deck (now a vertical surface) until about half way through your dive, and then return along the port rail to the buoy line and make your ascent. Boat divers, remember where you started the dive to avoid getting back on the wrong boat at the end of your dive. It happens all too often, and can frighten everyone on your own boat when the group comes up one or two divers short!

The *Hooker* is intact and has most of her running gear still in place. She rests with her starboard rail on the bottom at about 95 feet (29 m) and the highest part of her port rail at about 60 feet (18 m). The stern and propeller point north. Blue and midnight parrotfish are often seen on the upper surface of the hull, feeding on the fuzzy algal growth. Their teeth marks can be recognized as small parallel scrapes.

Caution. Although you can get as deep—or deeper—at other places on Bonaire, most other sites have sloping profiles that encourage you to work your way upward gradually into shallow water toward the end of a dive. By comparison, your entire dive will be below 60 feet (18 m) while you're on the *Hooker*. Perhaps as a result of this kind of "square" profile, a disproportionate number of cases of decompression sickness have resulted from dives on the *Hooker*. Therefore watch your dive time, and don't forget to make a safety stop! In addition, although most hatches and doorways are open, the ship's interior should not be entered by anyone not trained in wreck penetration, and not carrying the specialized equipment necessary.

Don't Miss the Reef. Nearly everyone going to the *Hooker* overlooks the surrounding sand flat and reef, which offer decent diving, especially when the *Hooker* is crawling with divers. The garden eels near the wreck see a lot of divers, and tend to be less skittish and easier to photograph than many other garden eel colonies. If things get too crowded on the wreck, check out the nearby shoreward slope or the ridge seaward of the vessel.

10. THE LAKE (S)

DEPTH:	INNER REEF 50-80 FEET (15-24 M)
	OUTER REEF 60-130 FEET (18-40 M)
ACCESS:	BOAT OR SHORE
PARK SITE:	7

This site, also called Lake Bowker in honor of Bruce Bowker, features spectacular mountainous star coral on the outer reef.

Directions. The Lake is just south of Punt Vierkant, between Flamingo Airport and the salt works. If you're diving from shore, the buoy may be seen before you get to the antennas of Trans World Radio. The Lake is the first site north of the closely-spaced buoys over the wreck of the *Hilma Hooker*.

The Dive. The mooring for The Lake is in about 30 feet (9 m) of water, near the seaward edge of a shallow shelf. Snorkeling on the shelf is similar to that over Angel City and Alice in Wonderland: plenty of large sea fans, fire coral, feeding parrotfishes and tiny damselfishes guarding their turf. Cornetfish and trumpetfish are also common here.

Seaward of the shelf, there is a fairly steep, coral-covered drop-off to a white sand flat between 60 and 75 feet (18-23 m) deep. The sand flat (a "lake" of sand, hence the name) is bordered on its seaward side by a second reef parallel to the first. If you look seaward across the sand flat, you should be able to see the second reef on a clear day. The

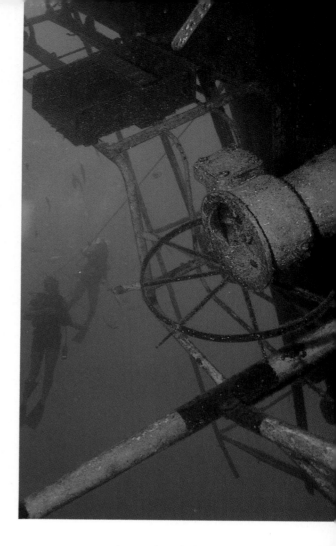

The auxiliary helm is one of the many interesting features to photograph on the wreck of the Hilma Hooker. *Photo: George Lewbel.*

second reef has a narrow crest that rises to about 60 feet (18 m) at its shallowest, and then plunges downward. It crosses sandy terrain beginning at about 130 feet (40 m), and then continues into the depths. The first reef has decent but somewhat ordinary diving. On the other hand, the second reef is outstanding. Huge heads of mountainous star coral form columns and stacks, and you're likely to see gigantic tiger groupers and a big barracuda or two on each dive.

11. PUNT VIERKANT (S)

DEPTH:	INNER REEF 30-90 FEET (9-27 M)
	OUTER REEF 70-120 FEET (21-36 M)
ACCESS:	BOAT OR SHORE
PARK SITE:	8

Punt Vierkant is the northernmost of the double-reef complex that begins with Alice in Wonderland.

Directions. Punt Vierkant is south of Kralendijk along the coastal road to the salt works. There is a small lighthouse adjacent to a cement pier marking the point. The buoy for Punt Vierkant is slightly south of the pier. Another landmark is the driveway to the Lighthouse Beach Resort.

The Dive. The sandy beach in front of the resort is an ideal entry and exit spot. The shallow shelf near the buoy, which is moored in about 20 feet (6 m) of water, has a lot of large gorgonians and staghorn coral colonies, and is very similar to the shelf at other nearby sites such as The Lake and Angel City.

Seaward of the buoy, the inner reef starts at about 40 feet (12 m) and bottoms out at a sand channel at around 100 feet (30 m). Garden eels are often seen in the sand channel.

The outer reef on the other side of the sand channel is a low-lying ridge with a crest only 10–20 feet (3–6 m) above the sand. The seaward edge of this reef has some good basket sponges and gorgonians, and a few very large brain coral heads, but most of the larger corals and sponges are along the upper edge of the ridge.

We don't recommend that you drop very far down over the slope, even if you're curious about the seaward side of the outer reef. Alice in Wonderland has similar terrain in shallower water, and The Lake has a better outer reef. Punt Vierkant isn't as lush in general, and the outer reef starts so deep that when you get there, you're already likely to be running out of dive time and air. Instead, spend your time along the top of the ridge and above the sand channel. Toward the south (left, facing seaward), the ridge rises up into shallower water, and you're likely to see Nassau groupers, tiger groupers and large barracudas.

12. DEBBIE BOB (S)

DEPTH:	30-80 FEET (9-24 M)
ACCESS:	BOAT OR SHORE

Debbie Bob is known for its fish action, and is a good spot to make a night dive to see expanded basket stars feeding.

Directions. Drive south of Kralendijk along the coast road, but don't go as far south as the Trans World Radio towers. On the seaward side of the road, you'll see the Bonaire Sunset Villas, and a tennis court with four tall lights on poles. Take the road next to the tennis court over to the water. The small lighthouse for Punt Vierkant and the pier at the Villas and the Lighthouse Beach Resort will be visible on your left as you face the sea. The buoy for Debbie Bob should be a short distance to your right.

The Dive. The sand beach offers a very easy entry and exit point. The buoy is moored in about 30 feet (9 m) on a beautiful shelf which boasts a magnificent gorgonian bed, with huge waving sea fans. Many of the gorgonians have basket stars entwined around their branches. The shelf at Debbie Bob is an excellent choice for a night dive, though a wet suit is recommended because of the abundance of fire coral. The basket stars expand at night to feed, reaching up to 3 feet (1 m) in diameter.

Intense Fish Action. Fish action in shallow water at Debbie Bob can be intense, with big schools of juvenile bar jacks plunging in and out of gorgonians, yellow snappers looking for a handout, and goatfishes milling around on the bottom.

The edge of the shelf is at about 40 feet (12 m), and is not as abrupt as at many other sites. The slope down from the shelf is gentle, with some very large sponges. Coral cover is good on the slope at Debbie Bob, but the site is rightfully known best for its fish, which are most dense above 80 feet (24 m). The slope ends at around 110 feet (34 m) on a sandy bottom.

13. CHEZ HINES (S)

DEPTH:	25-110 FEET (8-34 M)
ACCESS:	BOAT

Excellent snorkeling and large orange elephant-ear sponges highlight Chez Hines.

Directions. There is no easy shore access to this site because it lies off private property. Chez Hines is two buoys north of Punt Vierkant, between Debbie Bob and Corporal Meiss.

The Dive. The shelf here is relatively shallow, extending seaward to about 25 feet (8 m), making it an excellent spot for snorkelers. Large sea fans, some fire coral, and plenty of parrotfishes, trumpetfish and goatfishes make the shelf similar to Debbie Bob.

Orange Elephant-Ear Sponges. The slope drops gently to the sand at about 100 feet (30 m). The most photogenic feature of the slope is its big orange elephant-ear sponges. Some of them are as large as the sponges on the west side of Klein Bonaire.

Seaward of the sand flat, there is a second low-profile coral reef, and a deep bed of gorgonians beginning around 110 feet (34 m). The sand flat drops off more rapidly into deep water on the seaward side of the gorgonian bed. The sand flat between the gorgonian bed and the base of the reef slope has a garden eel colony. Conch are sometimes seen on the shelf, as well as on the sand flat at the base of the reef. Horse-eye jacks are not uncommon at Chez Hines, and there seem to be quite a few resident tiger groupers.

14. CORPORAL MEISS (S)

DEPTH:	30-125 FEET
	(9-38 M)
ACCESS:	BOAT OR SHORE

Corporal Meiss has abundant goatfishes, yellow stingrays and some huge, spiked basket sponges.

Directions. To dive from shore, follow J.A. Abraham Boulevard southward from Kralendijk towards Flamingo Airport. Just before you come to the airport, the road will jog sharply to the left, then to the right at a small traffic circle, and again to the right along the northern side of the airport. When the road swings to the left to continue down the coast, you're almost there. You'll see a short dirt road leading to a concrete breakwater, and a sand and cobble beach off the tip of the runway. The buoy off that beach is Windsock Steep. The next buoy to the south marks Corporal Meiss. The buoys are very close to one another, and the same beach can be used for shore access to both sites.

The Dive. The shelf at Corporal Meiss is somewhat sandy, with large gorgonians, fire coral, elkhorn and staghorn coral, and a dense fish community. Goatfishes tend to be particularly abundant, along with yellow stingrays, parrotfishes, and the usual shallow water Bonaire species. The reef slope begins at about 30 feet (9 m), and drops gently down to a sand bottom at about 100 feet (30 m). It has good coral and sponge cover, and is inhabited by many small groupers, hinds, and angelfishes.

Spiked Basket Sponges. One of the most distinctive features of Corporal Meiss is its sponge community found on the sand at a depth of about 120–125 feet (36–38 m). Here you will find some trash-can-sized, maroon-colored basket sponges covered with long spikes! Try to resist touching them; they're fragile, and the spicules in the sponges may irritate your skin.

A crinoid and one of the large, multiple-vented barrel sponges in deep water at Corporal Meiss. Photo: Larry Martin.

15. WINDSOCK STEEP (S)

DEPTH:	25-110 FEET
	(8-34 M)
ACCESS:	BOAT OR SHORE
PARK SITE:	9

The shallow shelf of this site is a good spot for snorkelers to enjoy a variety of corals.

Directions. Windsock Steep is located directly off the approach end of the runway at Flamingo Airport. Follow the directions for the Corporal Meiss site to get to the shore entry for Windsock Steep.

The Dive. This site's buoy is moored in about 15 feet (5 m) of water on a shallow shelf. The terrain is very similar to that at Corporal Meiss. The shelf has elkhorn, staghorn and fire coral, and gorgonians. Mullet are often seen on the shelf. Even though it's sandy, snorkelers will enjoy seeing the fish life. Tiger groupers are sometimes seen in shallow water as are many kinds of parrotfish.

A lone barracuda keeps watch beneath the hull of a moored dive boat. Photo: George Lewbel.

The gentle reef slope starts at about 25 feet (8 m) and bottoms out at a sand flat around 110 feet (34 m) deep. The slope has good coral and sponge cover, but is a bit more sandy than at Corporal Meiss. This may be a benefit to those less experienced divers who sometimes need a safe place to rest on the bottom without damaging the reef. There is a garden eel colony on the sand flat near the base of the reef slope.

16. CALABAS REEF (S)

DEPTH:	30-110 FEET (9-34 M)
ACCESS:	SHORE
PARK SITE:	10

Tame fish, easy access and lighted entries make this reef ideal for night diving.

Directions. Calabas Reef is named for the Calabas Restaurant at the Divi Flamingo Beach Hotel, and lies directly seaward of it. The hotel is a short distance south of the new Town Pier, toward the southern end of Kralendijk.

The Dive. Access to Calabas Reef is via the sandy beach in front of the hotel, off the restaurant pier toward the northern end of the hotel, or off the pier at the Dive Bonaire facilities at the southern end of the hotel.

Because of its ease of access, Calabas Reef is an ideal training spot. Lights on both piers make them convenient for night dives, too.

There is no specific buoy marking Calabas Reef, although there are a number of mooring buoys near the edge of the shallow shelf. Snorkelers will find the sandy shelf comparatively barren in terms of coral, but the fish are well worth the trip. Mullet, goatfishes, blue tang, yellowhead jawfish, trumpetfish, red hinds, peacock flounders, and yellowtail snappers are abundant on the shelf, as well as the occasional bonefish. Tarpon are sometimes seen there, especially at night when they feed on small fish attracted to the hotel's lights. Barracudas usually lurk just beneath the hulls of moored vessels. The fish are so used to divers that they won't even get out of your way; they'll expect you to swim around them!

The reef slope begins at about 40 feet (12 m), and drops gradually down. It turns into isolated patches of coral and sea whips on sand at about 110 feet (34 m). Considering the number of dives made on the slope, the coral is in pretty good condition. Many spotted drums, eels, rock and red hinds, coneys, and small groupers live among the corals and sponges on the slope. Toward the northern end of the site, there is a small wreck at about 80 feet (24 m). Black crinoids often perch on top of the wreck, and several large morays call it home.

17. TOWN PIER

DEPTH:	20-40 FEET (6-12 M)
ACCESS:	BOAT OR SHORE
PARK SITE:	11

Pilings covered with orange cup corals make the Town Pier Bonaire's single most famous dive.

Directions. The Town Pier is next to the small fish market in downtown Kralendijk, near where Simon Bolivarstraat meets the water at Kaya J.N.E. Craane. Other nearby landmarks include the Zeezicht Bar and Restaurant (about a block to the north), and the Customs Office to the south. There are only three large piers in Kralendijk, all within a couple of blocks of one another, and the Town Pier is the northernmost.

Before the other piers were built, it was the only "Town Pier." Now, its official name is the North Pier (as opposed to the Roll-on, Roll-off ["Ro-Ro"] Pier next to it, and the South Pier). However, it is so well known to divers as the Town Pier that we've kept the name.

Some dive operators do run boats to the Town Pier, although it's a very easy shore dive. The best shore access is next to the little fish market building, recognizable by its classical-looking columns. During the day, fresh-caught fish are displayed there on stone tables. At night, the fish market is a comfortable place to gear up.

The Dive. The concrete boat ramp next to the fish market provides an easy entry and exit. Watch your step; the ramp can be slippery. Once off the ramp, swim over the sandy bottom toward the middle of the northern leg of the L-shaped pier. Be especially vigilant for fishing lines and hooks. The pier is a popular fishing spot for locals. Monofilament is nearly invisible underwater—especially in the dark—and may stretch from piling to piling. Make sure that both you and your buddy carry a knife or other line-cutting device and can reach it with either hand.

Orange Cup Corals. The Town Pier is at its best at night, though it can also be an interesting afternoon dive. Many of the pilings are covered with orange cup corals, which expand only in the dark. Among the cup corals, you'll find arrow crabs, sharpnose

---

PERMISSION TO DIVE TOWN PIER

The Town Pier is home to several ocean-going tugboats, and usually has at least a few other large vessels tied to it. Extreme caution diving around the pier is obviously required. The Harbormaster (located in the small cannon-equipped building to the south of the pier) has the authority to issue or deny permission to dive the Town Pier, but the office is usually closed in the evenings. Check during the day with the Harbormaster to obtain permission to dive the pier in the evening. If you're with one of the island's dive operators, ask that operator to assist you, or to make the necessary arrangements. In any case, you are now required to be accompanied on the dive by a divemaster or instructor from Bonaire. An additional caution: before you jump in, walk over to the tugboats (if at the dock) and ask one of the tug captains for an update. They nearly always know who's coming and who's going.

The two best places on Bonaire to see and photograph orange cup corals are beneath the Town Pier and the Salt Pier at night. Photo: Larry Martin.

puffers, filefishes, sponge-covered masking crabs, and hundreds of other small invertebrates. Big purple tube sponges hang into the water, trumpetfish pretend they're part of the pier, and lots of moray eels linger in the spare tires and other debris at the base of the pier. Thin-tentacled, white cerianthid anemones reach up from the sandy bottom. The lights on the pier attract schools of baitfish, as well as tarpons and other predators drawn in for a meal. It's likely that

more rolls of film have been shot here underwater after dark than anywhere else in the world!

On the swim back toward the fish market, keep an eye out for valuables that people tend to drop while they're fishing from a dock. If you'd like to see a few more eels, you've got a good chance along the base of the concrete seawall next to the boat ramp. There are some crevices in shallow water that often shelter morays.

18. SOMETHING SPECIAL

DEPTH:	10-90 FEET (3-27 M)
ACCESS:	BOAT
PARK SITE:	28

Also known as Playa P'abou, this site offers an abundance of scorpionfish and garden eels.

Directions. Something Special is located just south of the entrance channel to the marina. Shore access is restricted due to private property, so Something Special is most easily dived from a boat. The buoy is moored on a shallow sand flat about 10 feet (3 m) deep.

The Dive. Seaward of the buoy, there is a very steep wall that starts about 30 feet (9 m) deep, and falls off nearly vertically to a sloping sand bottom. The base of the wall is about 50 feet (15 m) deep at its northern edge, but slants downward to the left (facing the sea) into very deep water toward the south. The sand bottom at the base of the wall thus rises into shallow water on the north, and falls off into deep water toward the south. In addition, the sand bottom becomes deeper as you go seaward from shore.

Scorpionfish. For a highly diverse dive, follow a circular route. First, drop down the wall directly in front of the buoy. The wall has a large population of scorpionfish, and good sponge and coral cover. You should reach the sand bottom at the base of the wall at about 80 feet (24 m), at which point you should see a large colony of garden eels out on the sand.

Photo Tip. Since these eels are used to seeing lots of divers, they are harder to spook than many other garden eel colonies around Bonaire. You can usually sneak up for a photo by staying as close to the sand as possible, and freezing for a few moments if they start to retract back into their holes.

After visiting the garden eel colony, return to the wall, and turn left (northward). Continue to swim along the base of the wall, which will gradually become more shallow. If you're lucky, you may see mating cornetfish

that sometimes cluster on the sand, and large schools of yellow goatfish. Continue upward, hugging the wall. You'll soon be in very shallow water to the north of the buoy. In the shallows, keep your eyes open for mullet, yellow stingrays, and perhaps a few large tarpon. Before returning to the buoy, peek in some of the holes in the stone breakwater, and inside the abundant old tires on the bottom. Lobsters and eels are common there.

Caution. Due to the danger of vessel traffic, stay especially alert near the surface and do not enter the channel.

19. FRONT PORCH (S)

DEPTH:	30-120 FEET (9-36 M)
ACCESS:	SHORE
PARK SITE:	29

Located on one of the finest sand beaches on Bonaire, this site offers an assortment of reef fish along with snake eels and morays.

Directions. Front Porch is directly in front of the Sunset Beach Hotel (called by many locals by its former name, the Hotel Bonaire) just past the marina, a few minutes drive north of Kralendijk on the main road.

The Dive. Access to the dive site couldn't be easier. Just wade in and go diving. There is no specific buoy for the site.

Many classes have been taught on the sandy shelf at Front Porch, which has the usual assortment of sand-dwellers such as yellowhead jawfish, mojarras, lizardfishes, stingrays, and goatfishes. For more experienced divers, the reef slope begins at around 20 feet (6 m), and continues down to a white sand bottom at about 120 feet (36 m). There are a lot of large sponges, including many specimens of the "do-not-touch-me" variety, but not much in the way of coral. Snake eels and morays are especially common. Garden eels may be found on the deep sand flat at the base of the slope.

Caution. There is a lot of boat traffic in front of the hotel, so extra caution is recommended when near or on the surface.

Bluespotted cornetfish are often mistakenly identified as trumpetfish, but cornetfish are much longer. They reach about 6 feet (2 m) in length, and have a long, whiplike filament at the tips of their tails. Cornetfish are most often spotted cruising at high speed just above the bottom in sandy or grassy areas. Mating groups of cornetfish have been seen on the deeper parts of the slope at Something Special. Photo: George Lewbel.

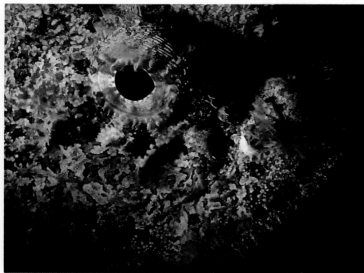

The spotted scorpionfish is thoroughly camouflaged to look like an algae-covered rock, and completes the illusion by resting motionless most of the time. Avoid being stung by its poisonous dorsal spines; stay above the reef, and look carefully before you touch anything even remotely resembling a stone. Photo: George Lewbel.

Garden eels live in sand burrows and face into the current to catch passing plankton. They are timid, but if you move towards them very cautiously, you may get near enough to see them darting their heads forward, picking out their tiny prey from the water. Garden eel colonies can be found at the base of many of Bonaire's slopes. They are also common on the seaward side of Klein, though in much deeper water. Photo: George Lewbel.

20. BARI REEF (S)

DEPTH:	30-130 FEET (9-40 M)
ACCESS:	SHORE

The well-lit dock at the Sand Dollar Beach Club is an ideal place to make a night dive and see tarpon.

Directions. This site is located in front of the Sand Dollar Beach Club, just past the Sunset Beach Hotel on the road north of town.

The Dive. Entry is by a giant stride directly off the dock in front of the Sand Dollar Dive and Photo which shares the dock with the Green Parrot Restaurant, a great place to relax after your dive. There are also stairs which offer an easy (though sometimes slippery) exit or an alternative entry. Fresh water showers and convenient freshwater rinse tanks are available on the dock.

The shelf here is sandy and deepens gradually from about 10 feet (3 m) by the

Peacock flounders are usually gray or tan with brilliant blue spots, but they can become mottled to match their surroundings on a moment's notice. Photo: George Lewbel.

dock to about 30 feet (9 m) where the gradual slope begins approximately 125 feet (38 m) from shore. This area is a great place for divers to acclimate themselves, and the pool-like conditions are perfect for training dives.

To the south, the shallow zone is dominated by sponges of all colors and sizes. On the northern portion of the shallows, elkhorn, brain, fire and pillar corals are common. Throughout the shallows, parrotfishes, peacock flounders, trunkfish and French angels abound. A sharp eye may even spot an octopus or frogfish.

Typical fish on the slope include rock and red hinds, schools of schoolmaster snappers and grunts, sharptail snake eels, creole wrasses, damselfishes, and blue and brown chromis. The upper slope is dominated by star corals, purple tube sponges and azure vase sponges, gradually giving way to plate corals and barrel sponges in deeper water. The slope ends in sand at about 130 feet (40 m) where there is a colony of garden eels.

Tarpon. This is an excellent spot for a night dive. All along the slope are many sponges where you can watch the snake eels and spotted morays searching the tubes for the small invertebrates that hide there. Tarpon are often seen here, attracted by divers' lights and the lights on the dock. Often, they will swoop in close to divers and snatch small fish

caught in a diver's light beam. Tarpon get large, and can be a bit unnerving when you are not expecting them, but they are harmless to divers.

Don't overlook the rock jetty near the dock at the end of your coral dive. It is a good place to see spiny lobsters, red coral shrimp and sleeping parrotfishes encased in their cocoons.

Caution. There is some boat traffic in front of the dock, so be on the lookout when on or near the surface. There are large roped off areas protected from boat traffic for carefree snorkeling. In these areas, there are rafts for resting and sunning.

21. LA MACHACA (S)

DEPTH:	30-130 FEET (9-40 M)
ACCESS:	SHORE
PARK SITE:	30

The reef here is in good shape and features two sunken vessels, La Machaca and the Hesper.

Directions. This site is in front of dive facilities at Captain Don's Habitat, north of the Sand Dollar Beach Club along the main road. The site is named for the remains of the La Machaca.

The Dive. Access is easy. Walk to the end of "Baby Dock," the shorter of Habitat's piers ("Papa Dock" is used for loading dive boats), and step in. Be careful not to hit the bottom; the shelf near the pier is about 6 feet (2 m) deep, depending on the tide. There are steps that can be used for an exit, but be cautious as they are usually slippery.

The shallow shelf is fairly sandy in front of Habitat, but snorkeling is excellent to the north of the hotel (right, facing the water). There are massive elkhorn and staghorn corals, and a lot of fire coral. It would not be out of the ordinary to see puffers, nudibranchs and mullet there.

A large line on the bottom leads from the dock down the reef slope, which begins at a depth of about 30 feet (9 m). The line passes near the remains of the La Machaca, a small fishing boat that Captain Don sank there many years ago. It rests near the lip of the slope at about 35 feet (11 m) and usually has a few crinoids perched atop its inverted hull. The line also serves as a navigational aid to help you return directly to the pier at the end of a dive. When you're halfway through your dive, come up into shallow water, turn back toward the point where you began your descent, and swim along the reef until you find the line. It will guide you to the exit.

There are many fish cleaning stations near the crest of the slope. Grunts and snappers tend to hang around the large gorgonians, waiting to be cleaned by wrasses and other small fish. The slope is covered with coral and sponges, and there is some black coral near the base of the slope. Scorpionfish, peacock flounders and rock hinds are abundant. Divers often report seeing sea snakes crawling along the bottom there, not knowing that they have been fooled by the wily snake eel, a harmless beast that lives on tiny crustaceans.

The slope ends on sand at about 130 feet (40 m), where a medium-sized garden eel colony and an occasional ray await deeper divers. Farther to the north on the sand is the 50-foot (15 m) Hesper, a Venezuelan fishing boat. It is still pretty bare, having been sunk there recently. However, it has an interesting structure with large square beams, and is home to a huge green moray. If dive time is a factor, the Hesper probably is not worth the decompression obligation you're likely to incur at that depth.

22. CLIFF (S)

DEPTH:	25-70 FEET (8-21 M)
ACCESS:	BOAT OR SHORE
PARK SITE:	31

A vertical wall—one of the few in Bonaire—covered with orange ball anemones, wire coral and black coral is the highlight of this site which is also known as Flagpole.

Directions. Cliff is located in front of the Villas at Captain Don's Habitat, just north of the *La Machaca* site. The reef between *La Machaca* and Cliff is more or less continuous. Like many Bonaire and Klein Bonaire dive sites, there is no distinct boundary or break in terrain between sites. Divers in good physical condition often visit both sites on a single dive by jumping in at *La Machaca*, swimming down to Cliff, and returning via the underwater dive flag (see below) to *La Machaca*.

The Dive. There are steps between the Villas, and a sandy beach for exits and entries. The mooring at Cliff is anchored on the shallow shelf in about 10 feet (3 m) of water. The shelf is narrow, but offers snorkelers a lot of large elkhorn and staghorn coral to see. Keep an eye out for nudibranchs on the coral, puffers and the occasional octopus. There is also quite a bit of fire coral on which fire worms frequently crawl.

Vertical Wall. At about 30 feet (9 m), the shelf ends abruptly in a concave vertical wall that drops straight down to a terrace at about 70 feet (21 m). The wall has many orange ball anemones, long wire coral, and black coral colonies. The wall is often used as a training aid for divers who need experience in buoyancy control on vertical drop-offs, since (unlike many other vertical walls) it has a definite base that is not too deep. Below the terrace, the reef continues downward to a sand bottom at about 140 feet (43 m), but the most interesting characteristic of the site is the vertical wall, an uncommon topographic feature on Bonaire and Klein Bonaire.

Memorial. There is a unique underwater memorial near the edge of the shelf in about 25 feet (8 m) of water, a bit south of Cliff. A concrete block supports a tall pole that flies the red-and-white dive flag at half-mast. A bronze plaque provided by the Boston Sea Rovers dedicates the memorial as a tribute to previous underwater pioneers and explorers who have made that Final Dive.

23. SMALL WALL (S)

DEPTH:	40-100 FEET (12-30 M)
ACCESS:	BOAT OR SHORE
PARK SITE:	32

A vertical wall with some large sponges, plate and sheet coral, and a small cavern at its base makes this site an interesting dive.

Directions. Small Wall is accessible from shore via the pier at the Black Durgon Hotel, north of Kralendijk. To get there, drive along the coast road. You'll go past Captain Don's Habitat, the large, gray desalination plant, and then enter a small residential area. You'll soon see the Black Durgon on the seaward side of the road. There is also a mooring on the wide, shallow shelf at a depth of about 15 feet (5m).

The Dive. The easiest entry is to jump off the pier where there is a sandy shelf with some large gorgonian beds. Right next to shore, there is an interesting thin band of elkhorn and staghorn corals, and fire coral. Out on the shelf, snorkelers will often see lizardfishes, goatfishes, parrotfishes, barracudas and sand tilefish. The edge of the shelf is about 30 feet (9 m) deep. Schools of creolefish and creole wrasse usually feed on plankton in open water above the edge of the shelf.

Seaward of the shelf and to the south of the mooring, there is a short vertical wall. It is similar in size to the wall at Cliff, dropping from about 40 feet (12 m) to 80 feet (24 m). Unlike the wall at Cliff, however, it curves outward at its center and is closer to shore at its two ends. The wall has good wire corals and some large sponges, as well as black coral and some plate or sheet corals. At night, orange ball anemones project from several crevices on the wall. There is a little cavern at the base of Small Wall. The bottom of the wall ends in a more gentle reef slope downward, which has good coral cover, especially in its deeper portions. Plate corals are abundant in the 100-foot (30 m) range; the slope bottoms out gently on white sand at depths over 130 feet (40 m). There is a large garden eel colony in the sand.

24. PETRIE'S PILLAR

DEPTH:	20-120 FEET (6-36 M)
ACCESS:	BOAT OR SHORE
PARK SITE:	33

The main attraction here is a beautiful head of pillar coral.

Directions. Petrie's Pillar is located along the northern road to Karpata. Shore access is via a left turn on a short, unmarked driveway about a mile north of the desalination plant. A numbered, yellow stone along the road marks the spot.

The Dive. Access from the cobble beach is through gaps in elkhorn coral, and there is a real potential for getting shredded if the surf's up, or you're careless.

Pillar Coral. Petrie's Pillar is a popular dive because there is a beautiful head of pillar coral just inshore and north (right, facing the sea) of the buoy mooring, in about 20 feet (6 m) of water. The pillar coral is showing some signs of damage due to handling by thousands of divers, so please admire it or shoot it—wide angle recommended—but don't bump it or sit on it. After all, it's the main attraction! There are also some outstanding sheets of fire coral near the pillar.

The mooring is about 35 feet (11 m) deep. The shelf inshore of the pillar is only marginally interesting. There is a lot of broken coral rubble there, and snorkelers won't find it particularly worthwhile. The coral on the slope is in good shape, especially in its deeper portions, although it is not particularly striking compared to other Bonaire dive sites. The slope begins at about 40 feet (12 m), and is covered with mountainous and cavernous star coral down to around 100 feet (30 m). The slope is a popular hangout for white-spotted orange filefish and scrawled filefish. The base of the slope has big stacks of sheet corals, extending downward from about 100 feet (30 m) toward a sand bottom at over 140 feet (43 m).

25. BARCADERA

DEPTH:	30-80 FEET (9-24 M)
ACCESS:	BOAT

Huge plate corals are found in relatively shallow water here.

Directions. Barcadera is located along the coast north of Kralendijk, between Petrie's Pillar and Oil Slick Leap. It has no easy access from the beach and the shelf is very narrow, making it a poor site for snorkelers.

The Dive. The reef slope at Barcadera begins seaward of the buoy at about 30 feet (9 m), and falls off gently to a sand bottom at over 130 feet (40 m). Its most interesting feature is huge colonies of plate corals in shallower water than at many other locations. If you're not interested in very deep diving but do want to see plate corals, Barcadera is for you. In fact, you'll be wasting precious dive time at Barcadera if you go deep; you can see it all in less than 80 feet (24 m) of water.

Most species of plate corals flourish in low-light environments where they can spread out like solar collectors. Their thin sheet-like colonies are too fragile to withstand wave shock, and they are abundant mainly below 100 feet (30 m) in most areas. However, at Barcadera, plate corals are layered upon one another like stacks of tan pancakes 6 feet (2 m) across, beginning in about 50 feet (15 m) of water. By the time you reach 70 feet (21 m), the slope is almost entirely covered with plate corals.

Photo Tip. Wide-angle setups are recommended for plate coral.

26. OIL SLICK LEAP

DEPTH:	30-130 FEET (9-40 M)
ACCESS:	BOAT
PARK SITE:	34

Moray eels and orange cup corals are abundant in shallow water along the rock wall.

Don't let the name put you off; there is no oil slick at Oil Slick Leap, but there is some very good diving. The site was named sarcastically in "honor" of a proposal to build an oil terminal near there some years ago.

Directions. The site between Barcadera and Thousand Steps has no easy beach access, despite the rusty ladder you'll see leading up the vertical cliff when you dive it from a boat.

The Dive. Below the water line, the cliff drops straight down 10 feet (3 m) to a shallow shelf. The shelf is too sandy to be interesting to most snorkelers, though there is some elkhorn and staghorn coral, and a thin band of gorgonians. The rock wall below the cliff along the shore has a lot of beautiful orange cup corals and quite a few moray eels in the holes at its base. A very large tiger grouper is often seen near a cavern in the wall, directly inshore of the buoy. The shelf near the rock wall is an excellent place to make a safety stop at the end of a dive.

The mooring is in about 30 feet (9 m) of water, near the edge of the shelf. The reef slope falls off gradually without a distinct break, and is made up of small ridges and valleys perpendicular to shore. The slope has good coral and sponge cover, extending at least as deep as 140 feet (43 m). Below 100 feet (30 m), large stacks of plate corals dominate the scene. Oil Slick Leap is a very good place to see morays and queen angels.

27. THOUSAND STEPS

DEPTH:	30-130 FEET (9-40 M)
ACCESS:	BOAT OR SHORE
PARK SITE:	35

This site, sometimes called Piedra Haltu, is good for fish watching, and its slope is densely covered with corals and sponges.

Directions. Thousand Steps is named for the stone stairway—not really a thousand steps, but enough to wear you out at the end of a long dive—leading from the beach to the coast road north of Kralendijk, on the way to Karpata. If you're diving from shore, there is a small parking space directly opposite the entrance to the Radio Nederland Wereldomroep (Dutch World Radio) antennas. You won't miss them as you drive north from town. The antennas are on the right side of the road, and they're big enough to see from miles away. Due to its easy shore access, Thousand Steps is often visited by snorkelers, but most of the good stuff is too deep to see from the surface.

The Dive. The beach is made up of cobbles and coral rubble, so watch your footing as you enter the water. The mooring is in about 20 feet (6 m) of water, a short distance from shore. The shelf around the mooring has a lot of gorgonians, and elkhorn and staghorn coral. The edge of the shelf is around 35 feet (11 m) deep, and has some very large mountainous star coral heads along its crest.

The slope is similar to that described for Ol' Blue and Karpata, two other nearby sites. The slope extends rather steeply downward to a sand bottom at about 150 feet (46 m). Coral and sponge cover on the slope is dense, with huge stacks of plate corals and flattened mountainous star coral on the lower reaches. Thousand Steps is a good choice for fish watching. You're likely to see a lot of tame animals, especially in shallow water. Spanish hogfish and queen angels will often come right up to you while you're making your safety stop or snorkeling.

The notch in the cliffs next to the road north of Kralendijk was cut by ancient waves when the sea level was much higher. You can observe the same process underway today where the present waterline meets the cliffs.

28. OL' BLUE (S)

DEPTH:	30-80 FEET (9-24 M)
ACCESS:	BOAT OR SHORE
PARK SITE:	36

Tame queen angels and Spanish hogfish, and huge purple "linguini" sponges up to 10 feet (3 m) across can be found at Ol' Blue.

Directions. To reach Ol' Blue, drive north past Thousand Steps and then slow down just after you pass the big radio antennas. If you pass Ol' Blue, you won't be able to dive it without going all the way back to Kralendijk and starting over, since the road is one-way to the north at that point. Keep your eyes open for the marker and a little coral rubble beach to your left in the center of a beautiful small cove.

The Dive. Right off the beach is good snorkeling with many gorgonian beds. The shelf ends at about 30 feet (9 m), and the reef slopes gently to about 60 feet (18 m). There is a second crest or break in the slope where the reef flattens out somewhat before resuming its downward angle, falling rather steeply to about 120 feet (36 m). Beyond this, plate corals dominate a fairly gentle slope that grades smoothly into a sand bottom at about 140 feet (43 m).

Gigantic Purple Sponges. The most distinctive feature of Ol' Blue is its gigantic purple "linguini" sponges, perhaps better known as finger sponges, though they don't look like fingers as much as they resemble a tangle of pasta.

Some of these sponges are up to 10 feet (3 m) across. The largest ones are found in the 60–80 feet (18–24 m) depth range, near the second crest. To find them, drop to about 60 feet (18 m) and maintain that depth contour as you swim along the drop-off in the center of the cove.

Photo Tip. To shoot the sponges, photographers will want to take a wide-angle lens along. Please don't handle the sponges or try to climb among the "branches" for a photo; they're fragile animals and are easily damaged. If you have a second camera, set it for macro shots since Ol' Blue is also famed for the world's tamest queen angels and Spanish hogfish, which sometimes come very close to divers.

29. BLOODLET (S)

DEPTH:	30-130 FEET (9-40 M)
ACCESS:	BOAT OR SHORE

Because Bloodlet is one of the less frequented sites, the reef is in excellent condition.

Directions. Bloodlet is located a short distance north of Ol' Blue. There is no easy land access over the ironshore, so the site is best dived from a boat.

The Dive. Snorkelers will enjoy working their way along the shelf next to the shore which has a pretty gorgonian bed, even though it is rather narrow.

Caution. Snorkeling is safe only on calm days; on rough days, waves are reflected back from the ironshore, producing a nasty surface chop that can make snorkeling hazardous and unpleasant.

The mooring on the shelf is near the start of the reef slope, in about 25 feet (8 m) of water. The slope has very heavy coral and sponge cover, broken by narrow sand- and coral-filled ravines perpendicular to shore. The reef has experienced comparatively few divers, and is still in a pristine state. Fish are still somewhat wary, meaning that you'll see more natural behavior, but you'll have to be sneaky to get a good photograph.

The reef at Bloodlet is more uniform than at many other sites, in terms of both its angle downward toward the sand bottom, and its reef structure. There are no obvious breaks in the slope or terraces to tip you off as to depth, and little clear-cut biological zonation. Toward the lower parts of the reef, the community becomes dominated by stacks of plate corals and long wire corals, which extend deeper than 170 feet (52 m) before tapering off into sand.

Caution. Keep an eagle eye on your instruments—it's very easy to get too deep at Bloodlet due to the lack of visual cues. The gentle slope downward goes on and on . . . .

30. RAPPEL (S)

DEPTH:	30-130 FEET (9-40 M)
ACCESS:	BOAT
PARK SITE:	37

Rappel is a spectacular dive with a cliff scarred by caverns and crevices cut by the waves.

Rappel is named for the technique used by early Bonaire divers to get to the site: rappelling down the sheer stone cliff below the road to Karpata. Rappel is dived exclusively by boat these days, unless you're the hardest of the hardcore.

The Dive. From the water, it's easy to see why the old-timers went to so much trouble to get there. Rappel's cliff drops vertically from the surface to a narrow shelf at about 30 feet (9 m). The cliff has been undercut by the waves, and has beautiful caverns and crevices. The mooring is within a stone's throw of shore, about 35 feet (11 m) deep. On a calm day, snorkelers will enjoy a close look at the lush underwater growth along the face of the cliff.

Caution. On rough days, the site is definitely not suitable for snorkeling.

If you prefer shallow diving, you might just stay up on the shelf and admire the rich assortment of cup corals, yellow pencil coral, green and spotted moray eels, and sponges living on and in the cliff. However, the water is likely to be a bit rough there, since incoming waves are reflected directly back out by the vertical wall, producing a surface chop most of the time.

Below the cliff, the slope falls off sharply, and is covered with mountainous and cavernous star corals, some black coral, and various other species. The terrain is rough, with prominent outcrops sticking out of the slope and projecting upward like small castles. The slope continues steeply downward to a sand bottom below 160 feet (49 m). There are backbone-like buttresses perpendicular to shore, and stacks of plate corals and wire corals in deep water.

31. LA DANIA'S LEAP

DEPTH:	30-130 FEET (9-40 M)
ACCESS:	BOAT OR SHORE
PARK SITE:	38

A long vertical wall and fields of steep buttresses make this site worth the walk if dived from shore.

La Dania's Leap is one of Bonaire's best deep dives. You can enjoy this site in shallow water, but if you're comfortable below 80 feet (24 m), you can get onto a genuine vertical wall.

Directions. While most diving at this site is by boat, there is shore access, but you've got to pay some dues. Take the road north of Kralendijk and stop your car as soon as you see the building for Karpata, several hundred yards farther along the one-way road. Unload all your gear and your buddy, carry your gear over the ironshore until you reach the edge, and then go park your car at Karpata. Walk back along the road toward La Dania's Leap until you see a little paved trail leading down toward the water. Stay to the right, rejoining your gear and your buddy.

The landing zone is a narrow gap between the coral heads directly shoreward of the buoy, at the base of the leap. It's only about 6 feet (2 m) down to the waterline, though it looks much farther when you're geared up!

Spotted morays are fairly timid, spending most of their time partially hidden beneath coral heads. After dark, they come out and hunt smaller fish on the reef. You'll have to go night diving to get a complete, full-length view. Photo: George Lewbel.

Caution. Once you jump, you're committed. There is no exit at La Dania's Leap. You'll have to swim to Karpata to get out.

The Dive. There is a mooring in about 20 feet (6 m) of water on the shallow shelf at La Dania's Leap. The shelf has a good gorgonian bed near its outer edge, but is fairly barren near shore with a lot of coral rubble. The reef slope begins at about 30 feet (9 m) deep, and falls off sharply into a field of steep buttresses separated by sand valleys. This buttress field continues to either side of the site extending all the way west to Karpata and most of the way east to Rappel. Sponge and coral cover is good on the buttresses, which are reminiscent of some of the sites on the south side of Klein Bonaire such as Forest and Hands-Off.

Vertical Wall. The vertical wall starts at the bottom of these buttresses. The top of the wall begins in comparatively shallower water to the east of the mooring (left, looking seaward), and becomes deeper to the west. The wall on either side of the mooring has a lot of black coral, wire coral, and plate corals. Large sponges project from the wall, and you're likely to spot fairy basslets and blackcap basslets hanging upside-down under ledges.

East of the mooring, the vertical wall starts at about 80 feet (24 m) and drops straight down to about 120 feet (36 m). It then eases into more gentle buttresses and valleys that continue into the depths. West of the mooring, the buttresses continue into deeper water. The vertical wall begins at about 100–125 feet (30–38 m), and drops to 150 feet (46 m). There are caverns and fissures near the base of the wall to the west of the mooring, but they're very deep.

The best way to dive La Dania's from shore is to descend to your maximum depth near the mooring, turn right (west), and work your way up-slope. When you get to about 35 feet (11 m), hold that depth contour and hug the wall. Continue westward until you see a grid of wires and lines. The grid was emplaced as a research project by the staff at Karpata Ecological Center. Don't give up—you're almost there. Turn up onto the shallow shelf, and exit via the steps at Karpata.

One of several old anchors resting just off the shelf at Karpata. Photo: Dave Brannon.

32. KARPATA

DEPTH:	30-80 FEET (9-24 M)
ACCESS:	BOAT OR SHORE
PARK SITE:	39

Karpata is one of the authors' personal favorites. It marks the northern end of the line for easily accessible shore sites along the leeward (west) coast of Bonaire and is frequented by pelagics. While two additional northern Bonaire sites are described, they are accessible only via the dirt roads in Washington/Slagbaai National Park. At Karpata, the paved road turns inland heading for the town of Rincón.

Directions. Karpata is across the street from the Karpata Ecological Center, a research and office facility operated by the Netherlands Antilles National Parks Foundation (called STINAPA). You will come to the Center on the right after driving north past La Dania's Leap. You can visit the Center, which is in a restored plantation house, but there are few exhibits for the public. There is a small parking area across the road from the stone steps on the seaward side of the road which lead down to a small rock and coral rubble beach.

The Dive. From the beach, swim through the channel in the elkhorn coral and out onto the shelf—be careful, the channel is narrow and shallow. The shelf experiences quite a bit of surf, since it is far enough out of the lee of Klein Bonaire to be exposed to weather from the south. Consequently, much of the coral on the shelf is periodically smashed by storms.

There is a park mooring about 10 feet (3 m) deep near several old ship anchors. To find the anchors, go straight offshore to the edge of the shelf, which is about 35 feet (11 m) deep. Turn left (eastward) and stay on the rim. You'll soon come to a massive double-fluked anchor partially embedded in coral at about 40 feet (12 m). There are at least two other anchors nearby, though they are more difficult to find. The anchors were probably placed on the reef intentionally for the use of ships that were moored at Karpata while taking on local plantation goods. Farther east, you'll find a STINAPA research grid of wires and lines fastened to the bottom, dividing part of the reef into small rectangles for detailed studies.

The slope below the anchor consists of nearly vertical buttresses and canyons that are heavily covered with coral and sponges. The base of the buttresses is at about 100 feet (30 m), below which they become less steep, but are covered by plate coral stacks down to at least 130 feet (40 m). The reef is most spectacular above 80 feet (24 m).

Karpata is well known for its fish life. Many pelagics are seen at Karpata, along with the usual suite of reef fishes. It's easy to find cleaning stations along the crest of the slope. Just look for a small ball of fishes milling around in one spot. Chances are good that there will be a larger fish in the middle, getting cleaned.

33. PLAYA BENGÉ

DEPTH:	35-100 FEET (9-30 M)
LEVEL:	VERY EXPERIENCED
ACCESS:	BOAT OR SHORE
PARK SITE:	43

Playa Bengé is a secluded bay with large spur-and-groove formations hosting an impressive array of fishes.

Directions. This site is up the coast from Karpata in Washington/Slagbaai National Park. The roads are not paved, and during much of the year are not passable. Rain turns parts of the Park into mud wallows, which remain as traps for unwary tourists in rental cars. By the way, some car rental contracts forbid travel on unpaved roads.

PRISCA'S SPECIAL ICE CREAM

From Karpata, you can't retrace your route back toward Kralendijk because the road is one-way northward. You'll have to take the inland road through Rincón, a small and beautiful old town. The road leaves the coast at Karpata, goes eastward over a hill with a fine view of the white church in Rincón, and then drops sharply into town. Be sure to make a stop at Prisca's Special Ice Cream shop.

To find Prisca's, turn left immediately before you get to the Amstel Bar, take the first left at Verona Bar Restaurant, go one block to a dip in the road, and take the left at the big yellow and white wall. Prisca's is the pink and green building. You can't miss it, unless you go on Wednesday when it's closed. Ask about the flavor of the day. It's often weird, and always good.

For a post-dive, post-drive treat, be sure to ask Prisca about the special of the day at her ice cream store in Rincón. Photo: Larry Martin.

In the north of Bonaire, the rugged hills of Washington/Slagbaai National Park are in sharp contrast to the lowlands of the south.

To get to Playa Bengé, follow the signs leading from the town of Rincón to the Park entrance. Entry fees are about $2 per person, and several interesting guide booklets and a map are available. Get the map, since some Park roads are unmarked. Ask directions, and in particular, confirm that the road to Playa Bengé is driveable.

Access to the small bay is over a dry lake bed (*salina*) that can turn to mud during the rainy season and become impassable to vehicles. If you do drive, close your car windows as this area is protected from wind and the insects will quickly find you. The entry is a few minutes walk from the parking area.

Caution. Occasional surf and strong currents can be found at this site. We strongly advise you not to dive if the conditions are adverse. There are plenty of alternative sites further south that are protected. Come back when the conditions are more favorable for a safe and enjoyable dive.

The Dive. Entry is over the coral rubble beach directly off the dry lake bed. Swim slightly north (right facing seaward) and you will soon be over a section of large spur-and-groove formations. The most impressive array of fishes is found in this area and includes many groupers, glassy sweepers in the protected undercuts, and schools of grunts and mahogany snappers. Schooling squid can sometimes be seen near the surface.

If you continue swimming seaward for about 10 minutes, you will come to the drop-off which starts at a depth of about 35 feet (11 m). Colonies of gorgonians can be found along this shelf. The coral-covered wall slopes moderately to a sand terrace at about 100 feet (30 m). Further north, a more vertical wall drops to around 160 feet (49 m). This area, however, isn't as interesting as the spur-and-groove section, and there are better deep dives elsewhere on the island.

At the bay entrance tarpon are commonly seen, and eagle rays and turtles are occasional visitors. Manta rays and schools of hammerheads have also been known to frequent this site.

To the south is a smaller spur-and-groove formation which is not as interesting for divers, but is fine for snorkelers.

34. BOCA BARTÓL

DEPTH:	30-80 FEET (9-24 M)
LEVEL:	VERY EXPERIENCED
ACCESS:	BOAT OR SHORE
PARK SITE:	41

Boca Bartól is one of Bonaire's most spectacular dives. It is a wide-mouthed cove with a magnificent spur-and-grove reef.

Directions. Boca Bartól is in Washington/Slagbaai National Park along the same unpaved roads as Playa Bengé but farther to the north. Check to insure the road to the site is open.

Caution. Spend a few minutes watching the water before you decide whether to get in. If swells are running, or there is any breaking surf, we strongly advise you to skip this dive no matter how rough and tough you may feel. On a bad day, you're likely to get pulverized in the surf line, and/or carried out to sea. Even if the surface appears calm, be very careful about currents, especially toward the outer part of the cove. If you encounter stronger water movement as you get farther from shore, return to the shallows and abort the dive if necessary. Typical current direction is from south to north across the mouth of the cove, i.e., away from Bonaire into the open ocean!

The Dive. The easiest access to the spur-and-groove formation is via the small beach at the southern end of the cove. There are several obvious access channels through the coral near shore. The spurs are long rows of parallel ridges perpendicular to shore. The grooves between them are filled with white sand. The spurs are about 30 feet (9 m) deep at their seaward bases, and they extend nearly to the surface. The northern side of the cove is more sandy, with a lower profile reef structure and a few large coral outcrops much farther offshore in very deep water. We recommend staying toward the south; an outstanding dive can be made without ever leaving the spur-and-groove formation.

These plate corals are growing in one of the spur-and-groove channels at Boca Bartól. Photo: George Lewbel.

The spurs are covered with coral and sponges, and crevices along their lower edges provide hiding places for morays and soapfishes. Massive sea fans are found on top of the spurs. The grooves shelter large fish that are relatively uncommon elsewhere on Bonaire, such as big groupers, horse-eye jacks, southern stingrays, tarpon, and blue and midnight parrotfish.

Sand Cascades. The bottom is sandy for a considerable distance seaward of the spurs and grooves. If there is no current, it's worth the 5- to 10-minute swim to the edge of the reef slope, which begins at about 55 feet (17 m). It is fairly barren in terms of coral cover, but has eerie sand cascades flowing down the slope into very deep water. Out on the sand, you'll see hermit crabs, foraging snappers and bar jacks, porgies, peacock flounders, rays, mullet, sand tilefish, and many other creatures that prefer sand habitats. The slope is covered with big chunks of coral that have been broken in shallow water and rolled downhill.

KLEIN BONAIRE SITES

All Klein Bonaire sites must be reached by boat. It's usually about 10 minutes across the channel from Kralendijk, though the trip may take as much as half an hour in bad weather.

35. JUST-A-NICE-DIVE

DEPTH:	20-120 FEET (6-36 M)
ACCESS:	BOAT
PARK SITE:	12

The long sand valleys of this site, which is also called Kanal, are paralleled on both sides by beautiful solid coral ridges.

Just-a-nice-dive is located on the east end of Klein Bonaire, facing Kralendijk.

The Dive. There is almost no shallow shelf, meaning that snorkelers will have little to see here. The slope starts right next to the shore, and drops steeply downward into the deep blue channel between Klein Bonaire and Bonaire. The mooring for the site is located in deeper water than usual—about 85 feet (26 m)—so that boats attached to the buoy don't swing into the shoreline.

The main attractions of the site are long, wide sand valleys that plunge into the abyss, flanked by parallel bands or strips of solid coral. You will probably find lots of peacock flounders and lizardfishes on the sand. The best coral is to the left (facing the sea) as you descend along the main valley in front of the mooring. The ridge on the left is solidly covered with orange sponges, pencil coral, club finger coral, cavernous star coral, and plate corals in deeper water. Big "bushes" of black coral are easy to find below 100 feet (30 m).

Just-a-nice-dive is an excellent place for a deep training dive. You can stay over sand while you're adjusting your buoyancy on descent, track to the left (north) at your maximum depth to see deep-water corals and sponges, and then ascend along the band of coral and return to the mooring.

36. BONAVENTURE

DEPTH:	40-130 FEET (12-40 M)
ACCESS:	BOAT

This site's terraced slopes make a dramatic profile for silhouette photographs.

Bonaventure is on the southern side of Klein, toward its eastern end. Its wide, shallow sand flat may not interest most snorkelers, but it is a fine location for a deep dive due to its dramatic, terraced profile and abundant fauna in deep water.

The Dive. The mooring is in about 20 feet (6 m) of water, half-way to the edge of the shelf. The reef slope begins at about 30 feet (9 m) with a steep drop from 40 feet (12 m) to about 80 feet (24 m). In some places the slope, which has dense coral and sponge cover, is nearly vertical. Below 80 feet (24 m) the slope flattens out somewhat and then "stair-steps" down into deep water with narrow terraces at several depth levels. Starting around 100 feet (30 m), large stacks of plate coral extend to about 150 feet (46 m) below which there is a sloping sand bottom.

TOUCH THE SEA

If you're interested in knowing more about reef biology, and the distribution and behavior of reef inhabitants, consider making a dive with Dee Scarr. Her Touch the Sea Program offers personalized dive guide service to specific locations where Dee has made hundreds of dives, and gotten to know many of the animals on a first-name basis. For a preview, catch Dee's free underwater slide show, presented nearly every week at Habitat. It's currently scheduled for 8:45 P.M. on Monday nights. Check with Habitat (phone 8290) to make sure the show schedule hasn't changed. To arrange a dive with Dee call her directly at 8529.

37. MONTE'S DIVI (S)

DEPTH:	40-130 FEET
	(12-40 M)
ACCESS:	BOAT

Also known as Divi Tree, this site boasts some of Klein's largest mountainous star coral heads.

Monte's Divi is between Bonaventure and Bonheur de Betsy, on the southern side of Klein Bonaire.

The Dive. The mooring in the middle of the shelf is about 25 feet (8 m) deep. The edge of the shelf is at around 40 feet (12 m), a bit deeper than at other nearby sites. Its shallow shelf is covered with a tangled mass of gorgonians, coral and finger sponges, making it one of the best locations on Klein for snorkeling. Snorkelers will see parrotfishes browsing on coral, huge schools of blue and brown chromis, trumpetfish, and many other reef-associated fishes. Seaward of the shelf, the reef slope drops evenly toward a sand flat greater than 150 feet (46 m) deep. The reef has a thriving coral and sponge community, and some of the largest mountainous star coral heads on Klein. Compared to the sites adjacent to it, the slope at Monte's Divi has a smooth, sheet-like topography without prominent breaks, terraces or ridges.

38. BONHEUR DE BETSY (S)

DEPTH:	30-130 FEET
	(9-40 M)
ACCESS:	BOAT

The Rock Pile, as this site is also named, is riddled with holes and hiding places for fish.

Bonheur de Betsy is between Monte's Divi and Joanne's Sunchi, on the southern side of Klein Bonaire. Despite its proximity to these other two sites, the reef at Bonheur de Betsy is very different from both of them.

The Dive. The mooring is in about 15 feet (5 m) of water near the edge of the shelf and snorkeling is good here. In the shallows, you'll find a mixture of sand, coral heads and gorgonians. Large schools of grunts and snappers are sometimes seen hanging still in the water, and herds of goatfishes and parrotfishes can be seen feeding on the shelf.

This lizardfish has a formidable set of teeth, as befits its one-strike predatory lifestyle. Lizardfishes rest camouflaged on the bottom or partially covered with sand, hiding from their prey. When smaller fish swim over, lizardfishes suddenly burst from cover and grab their victims. Photo: Dave Brannon.

The reef slope begins at about 20 feet (6 m) and drops steeply in a series of narrow steps or terraces, some of which have little sandy areas where you can rest without crashing on coral. The base of the reef is about 150 feet (46 m) deep, beyond which a sand flat continues to tilt sharply downward.

Tiger Groupers. Although the coral and sponges are in excellent condition, the main attraction at Bonheur de Betsy is its intense fish action. For instance, Bonheur de Betsy is one of the best places to find tiger groupers and other large fish.

39. JOANNE'S SUNCHI (S)

DEPTH:	30-130 FEET (9-40 M)
ACCESS:	BOAT

Both divers and snorkelers will enjoy the abundance of fish on the sandy shelf. Dramatic buttresses and sand cascades dominate the terrain at deeper depths.

Joanne's Sunchi (*sunchi* means "kiss" in Papiamento) is between Bonheur de Betsy and Captain Don's Reef, on the southern side of Klein Bonaire.

The Dive. Joanne's Sunchi is one of the most beautiful dives on the island. This site has a wide, shallow shelf with a mooring at about 15 feet (5 m). Even though the shelf is very sandy, it is highly recommended to snorkelers who want to see lots of feeding fishes. The sand flat supports large numbers of peacock flounders, sand tilefish, mojarras, bonefish, stingrays, bar jacks, trunkfishes and goatfishes, many of whom can be seen stirring up the sand, looking for smaller animals to eat.

Seaward of the mooring, steep ridges and sand channels begin at about 30 feet (9 m) and extend perpendicular to shore. The ridges or buttresses are covered with coral and sponges, extending to below 150 feet (46 m). Sand cascades flow down the valleys between them. Toward the bottoms of the ridges, stacks of plate corals and flattened mountainous star coral dominate the scene, along with wire corals more than 10 feet

(3 m) long. Big orange elephant-ear sponges can be found on the ridges. At the base of the ridges, a deep sand flat continues outward into very deep water.

Photo Tip. Photographers will definitely want wide-angle lenses here.

Plate and wire corals at Joanne's Sunchi. Photo: Larry Martin.

40. CAPTAIN DON'S REEF

DEPTH:	30-130 FEET (9-40 M)
ACCESS:	BOAT

Elephant-ear sponges and a variety of corals line the ridges of this site.

Captain Don's Reef is between Joanne's Sunchi and South Bay, on the southern side of Klein Bonaire. The site was named in May 1987 in honor of Captain Don Stewart's 25th anniversary on Bonaire.

The Dive. The mooring is anchored in 30 feet (9 m) of water on the edge of a magnificent drop-off. The narrow shelf inshore of the drop-off supports a bed of large gorgonians.

The slope below the drop-off begins with a series of steep terraces, whose sides become more gradual as depth increases. The topography consists of a series of parallel valleys and ridges perpendicular to shore. The valleys have sand channels down their centers, leading to a white sand flat at about 150 feet (46 m).

Elephant-Ear Sponges. The ridges are covered with big orange elephant-ear sponges, mountainous and cavernous star coral, and plate corals. Black coral and wire coral are abundant below 70 feet (21 m). Schools of blue and brown chromis and black durgon wheel above the lip of the drop-off.

41. SOUTH BAY (S)

DEPTH:	35-130 FEET (11-40 M)
ACCESS:	BOAT
PARK SITE:	14

Large fish, sponges and long wire coral accent this site.

South Bay is between Captain Don's Reef and Hands-off, on the southern side of Klein Bonaire. Its position is slightly out of the lee

Fan worms have fluffy crowns that function as gills and feeding structures. Microscopic cilia and mucus-filled grooves on the crowns catch and transport food particles to the mouth. They are light sensitive, and can detect shadows. For a close view, approach worms from below and don't shade them. Photo: Dave Brannon.

of Punt Vierkant. This exposes it to weather from the south, so it is usually rougher on the surface than at the more easterly sites.

The Dive. Sometimes there are moderate currents present here, usually toward the west, but eddies can cause reversals in current direction. The mooring at this site is in about 15 feet (5 m) of water surrounded by a shallow shelf with some scattered coral heads and a dense bed of gorgonians growing on a hard limestone pan. The reef slope begins at about 35 feet (11 m) and is fairly uniform in topography, forming a large, tilted sheet extending downward to a white sand bottom at depths greater than 130 feet (40 m). The reef has very good coral and sponge cover, and some high-relief mountainous star coral heads. Farther down slope, you'll find orange elephant-ear sponges, plate coral stacks and black coral. Closer to the base of the slope, long wire corals project outward amid some jumbo-sized black coral colonies.

Large fish are often seen at South Bay, including ocean triggerfish, scrawled filefish and schools of horse-eye jacks.

Sharksuckers do not confine themselves to the company of sharks. This one has found a green turtle to accompany for a while. Sharksuckers occasionally buddy with divers! Photo: George Lewbel.

42. HANDS-OFF

DEPTH:	30-130 FEET (9-40 M)
ACCESS:	BOAT
PARK SITE:	15

Hands-off has sand cascades, steep valleys and ridges.

Hands-off is one of the sites on the south side of Klein Bonaire, just east of Forest. It is exposed to more weather than the sites around the corner to the north, or the sites on the south side farther to the east. It was named Hands-off because when it was first established in 1981, photographers and novices were not permitted to dive here. The Bonaire Marine Park authorities were trying to determine whether or not camera-carrying divers, or those with imperfect buoyancy control, were harder on reefs than other divers. The experiment was discontinued almost immediately after it began because siltation and storm damage made it impossible to differentiate between the effects of diving compared with natural processes.

The Dive. Surface chop is typical and currents are sometimes strong, usually toward the west. The mooring is in about 20 feet (6 m) of water on a rather featureless shallow shelf covered with coral rubble and gorgonians. Seaward of the mooring, a spectacular reef slope begins in about 30 feet (9 m) of water. There is a broad, V-shaped valley directly below the mooring, with ridges on both sides. The valley is very steep near the top of the slope.

The slope at Hands-off is made up of a parallel series of buttresses and valleys resembling those at Forest. Some of the valleys at Hands-off have a considerable amount of sand in them, slowly cascading downward into deeper water, transporting broken bits of coral and algae from the shallows to the bottom. The upper portions of the buttresses are very steep, having several sharp pitches and narrow terraces. The ridges are covered with orange elephant-ear sponges and corals, and plenty of black coral.

Brain Corals. Plate corals and wire corals start at about 60 feet (18 m), and there are lots of huge brain corals in deeper water. Many of the brain corals have formed expanded sheets rather than the usual ball-like shape, so as to collect as much of the subdued light that is available at depth as possible. The reef slope bottoms out on white sand at about 150 feet (46 m).

Photo Tip. Photographers will want wide-angle lenses here.

43. FOREST

DEPTH:	30-130 FEET (9-40 M)
ACCESS:	BOAT
PARK SITE:	16

Forest is one of the authors' personal favorites for a deep dive due to its jagged topography, huge orange elephant-ear sponges and black coral colonies.

It is located on the south side of Klein Bonaire, between Southwest Corner and Hands-off. Because of the site's exposure, there is sometimes a surface chop at Forest and often moderate-to-strong currents, usually toward the west.

The Dive. The mooring is in about 20 feet (6 m) of water near the edge of a rather narrow shelf.

Seaward of the mooring, buttresses and valleys begin right at the edge of the slope which is about 30 feet (9 m) deep. Parallel ridges drop steeply to about 60 feet (18 m), and then angle downward more gradually. Some of the gulleys have sand channels in them leading to a sandy bottom at depths greater than 160 feet (49 m). If you plan to go deep at Forest, keep in mind that a gradual ascent along the ridges to the mooring may take a long time and a lot of air; their bases are quite far from the mooring.

Black Coral. Forest is named for its black coral colonies. You'll see them everywhere on the ridges, especially below 50 feet (15 m). To identify black coral, look for blackish-green bushes 3–5 feet (1–2 m) high. Mountainous star coral and huge orange sponges cover the ridges down to about 80 feet (24 m), where they are gradually replaced by stacks of deep-water plate corals up to 10 feet (3 m) across.

Even though the gulleys and ridges are spectacular, don't forget to look up from the bottom once in a while. Forest is a great place to see fish action. Scrawled filefish at Forest will get within camera distance of a diver, and it's not unusual to see jacks herding silversides or scad into a bite-size school for dinner.

Photo Tip. You'll want a wide-angle lens at Forest, since black coral colonies and sponges here are very large.

Close-up view of a giant brain coral. Photo: George Lewbel.

44. SOUTHWEST CORNER

DEPTH:	30-120 FEET (9-36 M)
ACCESS:	BOAT
PARK SITE:	17

A double-barreled barrel sponge is one of the unique attractions to be found here.

Southwest Corner is located (as you might suspect) at the southwest corner of Klein Bonaire, just around the block from Forest. Currents tend to be stronger at Southwest Corner than at most other sites, and dive guides tend not to take beginners here. It is not recommended for snorkeling unless currents are nil, even though the shelf is fairly broad and covered with coral.

The Dive. The mooring is in about 15 feet (5 m) of water. The reef slope begins seaward of the mooring at a depth of about 30 feet (9 m).

The slope at Southwest Corner is fairly uniform in topography, with a gradual descent into deeper water. It is covered with mountainous star coral, orange sponges and black coral. As depth increases, colonies of plate corals appear. The slope ends distinctly at a sand flat about 120 feet (36 m) deep. The sand flat is partially covered with a thin layer of algae, which gives it a strange gray appearance.

Double Barreled Sponge. If you follow the valley directly seaward of the mooring down to the deep sand flat and then turn left (facing away from Klein Bonaire's shore), you'll come to a unique, double-barreled barrel sponge at 120 feet (36 m). Back up the slope from the sponge and a bit to the south (right, facing the shore), there are some spectacularly photogenic eroded pillars of mountainous star coral in about 30 feet (9 m) of water. Looking upslope from the pillars, the mooring will be to your left.

Photo Tip. The barrel sponge and the pillars call for wide-angle lenses; they're bigger than you think.

45. MUNK'S HAVEN (S)

DEPTH:	30-100 FEET (9-30 M)
ACCESS:	BOAT

This site offers divers the opportunity to view the gentle "glow" of fluorescent sponges.

Munk's Haven is on the west end of Klein Bonaire, between Southwest Corner and Twixt. It is usually pretty calm, since most of the weather comes up from the south and Munk's Haven is tucked around the corner on the north side. Strong currents (usually toward the south) can sometimes be encountered here.

The Dive. The mooring is in about 15 feet (5 m) of water on a shallow shelf that offers excellent snorkeling, with big pinnacles of coral, large gorgonian sea fans and many fishes.

The reef slope begins at about 25 feet (8 m), and has very heavy coral and sponge cover. There are many highly eroded coral heads, most of which have orange cup corals inside their cavities. The slope is rather uniform in topography and falls steeply to a smooth sand bottom at about 130 feet (40 m).

Fluorescent Sponges. What makes Munk's Haven distinctive is not its coral, but its fluorescent sponges, most of which are in the depth range from 60-100 feet (18-30 m). Many of the fluorescent sponges appear to give off a gentle purple light. They are not actually glowing, but are absorbing ambient light and re-emitting it in a different wavelength.

Photo Tip. A brightly-lit strobe shot will not show this glow, but will produce an uninteresting photograph of a pinkish sponge. To show one in its true glory, keep your strobe power at a minimum, and expose for ambient light.

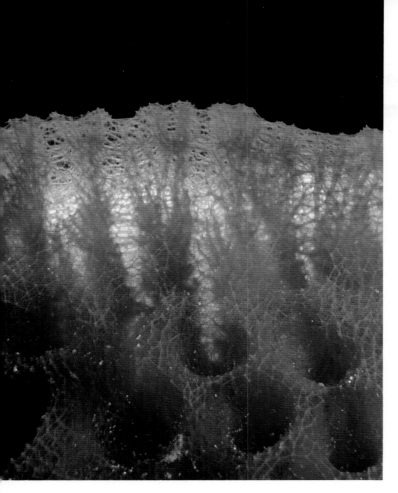

Fluorescent sponges are most abundant on the lower parts of coral-covered slopes below 60 feet (18 m). Fluorescent sponges absorb light in the blue end of the spectrum, and re-emit it in the red end, thus appearing to glow underwater. The best photographs of these sponges are taken using as little artificial light as possible. Bright strobes and video lights will produce tan-colored shots. Photo: George Lewbel.

In deep water at the base of the slope at Southwest Corner is this double-barreled barrel sponge. Photo: George Lewbel.

46. TWIXT (S)

DEPTH:	40-100 FEET (12-30 M)
ACCESS:	BOAT
PARK SITE:	18

A welcoming committee of yellowtails and queen angels looking for a handout will greet you at this site.

Twixt is located near the west (seaward) tip of Klein Bonaire, between Southwest Corner and Valerie's Hill. The current at Twixt is sometimes strong, usually toward the south.

The Dive. Twixt has traditionally been a popular fish-feeding spot, though this practice is slowly decreasing. Still, when you hit the water, you can expect to be mobbed by trained yellowtails and queen angels looking for a handout. We recommend that you stand them up unless you want to spend the rest of the dive fending them off.

The mooring is in about 20 feet (6 m) of water near the edge of a broad shallow shelf. The inshore part of the shelf has very good snorkeling, with many trumpetfish, queen angels and other relatively tame fish. The shelf is covered with scattered coral heads, big thickets of staghorn coral, large gorgonians and some dense patches of highly sculptured fire coral.

Orange Sponges. Beyond the shelf break which begins at about 30 feet (9 m), the slope drops off steeply to a sandy bottom at over 130 feet (40 m). Most of the better corals and sponges are in the 40- to 100-foot (12–30 m) range. On the slope, you'll find many of the very large orange sponges that are typical of the seaward side of Klein Bonaire. They get larger in deeper water, sometimes exceeding 6 feet (2 m) in length, sticking up 3 feet (1 m) above the bottom. Well-camouflaged, thumb-sized orange anemones are frequently embedded in these massive sponges. Above the slope, there are usually huge schools of blue and brown chromis feeding on plankton.

47. SHARON'S SERENITY (S)

DEPTH:	25-130 FEET (8-40 M)
ACCESS:	BOAT

Sharon's Serenity is probably the best snorkeling site on Klein, and also has vertical walls and good deep diving.

This site is just to the north of Twixt, on the west side of Klein Bonaire. Valerie's Hill is the next site north of Sharon's Serenity. The water here is normally fairly calm, though there can be currents present that move predominantly toward the south.

The Dive. The mooring is in about 20 feet (6 m) of water near the edge of the shelf. The shallow shelf at Sharon's Serenity is outstanding for snorkeling. It supports a bed of tall gorgonians, highly sculptured fire coral formations and a staghorn coral thicket. There are many parrotfishes and trumpetfishes, gray and French angels, and a prolific collection of damselfishes to be seen here.

Sharon's Serenity is a great place for a deep dive, though the base of the reef slope exceeds sport diving depths. It's also possible to do a wall dive here without getting into very deep water. The slope begins precipitously at the seaward edge of the shelf, about 25 feet (8 m) deep. It is covered with coral and sponges, and drops sharply downward in a series of narrow terraces parallel to shore. Between the terraces, there are several vertical drop-offs, so you have a variety of walls to choose from. The sand bottom at the base of the reef is at least 140 feet (43 m) deep. Wire corals and huge plate corals become prominent at about 80 feet (24 m), and are dominant below 100 feet (30 m).

Bottlenose Dolphins. Though we can't promise you'll be lucky enough to see them, bottlenose dolphins are often present at Sharon's Serenity in the afternoons.

48. VALERIE'S HILL (S)

DEPTH:	40-130 FEET (12-40 M)
ACCESS:	BOAT
PARK SITE:	19

After viewing the huge coral mounds at depth, divers can offgas on the shallow flat and watch nudibranchs and dueling parrotfishes.

Valerie's Hill is on the western side of Klein Bonaire. It is generally calm here; when a current is present, the usual direction of water movement is toward the south.

The Dive. The mooring on the shelf is in about 20 feet (6 m) of water. This shelf has a lot of fire and staghorn coral, and is an excellent place for snorkelers to spot nudibranchs. Parrotfishes frequently chase each other around on the shelf, dueling for food and territory.

Seaward of the mooring, the reef slope begins with large heads of mountainous star coral at about 40 feet (12 m). The slope is fairly steep, somewhere between Twixt (flatter) and Sharon's Serenity (steeper) in angle of descent. It is covered with coral and sponges all the way down to a sandy bottom at over 130 feet (40 m). Huge coral mounds project upward from the slope. Below 80 feet (24 m), there are big stacks of plate corals, purple tube sponges and large, orange elephant-ear sponges. Schools of blue and brown chromis are always present, feeding on plankton above the reef.

Black-and-white crinoids are related to urchins and sea stars. They feed by removing plankton from the water. In search of water currents, crinoids sometimes crawl up to the tips of gorgonian or sponge stalks, or station themselves on top of coral heads. Photo: George Lewbel.

49. MI DUSHI (S)

DEPTH:	30-130 FEET (9-40 M)
ACCESS:	BOAT
PARK SITE:	20

The dramatic drop-off at this site, sometimes called Johanna's Revenge, reveals a forest of wire corals and large tube sponges.

Mi Dushi is located on the northwest side of Klein Bonaire, between Valerie's Hill and Carl's Hill. Along the shore is a small, sandy beach. Diving conditions are generally excellent, though it's not uncommon to have a bit of current, usually (but not always) toward the southwest. If the water is moving toward the northeast, you can sometimes talk a boat operator into following your bubbles in a drift dive from Valerie's Hill (the site south of Mi Dushi) through Mi Dushi, or even to Carl's Hill.

The Dive. The mooring at Mi Dushi is in about 25 feet (8 m) of water, near the edge of the shelf. Snorkeling is very good in water 10–20 feet (3–6 m) deep on the broad shelf, where you'll find plenty of parrotfishes, thickets of staghorn, elkhorn and fire coral. Below the shelf, the drop-off begins at about 30 feet (9 m) and falls off dramatically. Parallel buttresses and shallow valleys descend perpendicularly to shore, reaching a sand bottom at about 150 feet (46 m). Sand cascades are sometimes seen in the valleys, carrying sediment from the shelf to the bottom.

Large Tube Sponges. Prominent features of the reef slope at Mi Dushi include a forest of wire corals starting at a depth of about 60 feet (18 m), tangles of gorgonians and finger sponges 10 feet (3 m) wide, and gigantic purple tube sponges. You'll find a very large tube sponge by dropping down the slope from the buoy and swimming northeast (left, facing shore) for about three minutes, while maintaining a depth of about 60 feet (18 m). Please don't handle the sponges. They're starting to look frayed from too many divers touching them.

The wire corals in deeper water grow amidst enormous stacks of plate corals, which extend downward all the way to the base of the slope. The plate corals get larger and larger below 100 feet (30 m), and are well worth a trip if you've got the dive time and the air.

50. CARL'S HILL ANNEX (S)

DEPTH:	25-130 FEET (8-40 M)
ACCESS:	BOAT

Aggressor III, another name for this site, boasts a steeply sloping reef, and corals and sponges in near-perfect condition.

Carl's Hill Annex is toward the northern side of the west end of Klein Bonaire, just south of Carl's Hill.

The Dive. The mooring is in about 20 feet (6 m) of water on a beautiful shallow shelf covered with large sea fans and fire coral. On the shelf, you're likely to find anemones sheltered in broken coral rubble, tobaccofish, pipefish, Spanish hogfish, and, if you look very carefully, a sea horse or two.

The terrain at Carl's Hill Annex is similar to that at Mi Dushi, the adjacent site to the south: high relief and spectacular. There are nearly vertical buttresses and parallel valleys, beginning at about 35 feet (11 m) at the edge of the shallow shelf. The reef slope drops very steeply toward the sand bottom at its base, more than 130 feet (40 m) deep. Since the mooring was installed quite recently, the corals and sponges at Carl's Hill Annex are in nearly perfect condition.

The middle and lower parts of the slope have a lot of black coral and some orange elephant-ear sponges. Toward the base of the slope, long wire corals and plate corals take over.

This "smoking" purple tube sponge is pumping out a cloud of sperm, as are other nearby sponges. Many sponges spawn en masse. Their sperm cells are carried by water currents to other sponges that contain eggs waiting to be fertilized. This kind of long-distance sexual reproduction eventually produces a swimming larva, which settles elsewhere to begin a new colony. Photo: George Lewbel.

Klein Bonaire is noted for its fine purple tube sponges. Photo: Larry Martin.

51. CARL'S HILL (S)

DEPTH:	30-100 FEET (9-30 M)
ACCESS:	BOAT
PARK SITE:	21

This site, also called Punta P'abou, is best known for its vertical wall and diverse underwater topography.

Carl's Hill is next to the little point of land marking the northern end of the west side of Klein Bonaire. Many divers skip the wall and enjoy the more gentle adjacent slopes. This site is usually calm, but strong currents are sometimes present. They generally flow from east to west.

The Dive. The mooring is at about 25 feet (8 m) on a beautiful shallow shelf. Near the mooring, there is a gorgonian bed, and some thickets of staghorn and elkhorn coral, as well as a lot of fire coral. Spotted drums are common under coral heads on the shelf. The best snorkeling is near the mooring and to the southwest; toward the northeast, the shelf becomes quite narrow.

Adjacent to the mooring, the reef slope begins in about 35 feet (11 m) of water, and falls off steeply toward a sand bottom at about 130 feet (40 m). There are several narrow ridges and adjacent valleys running down the slope, which has dense coral cover and several large purple tube sponges, especially in the 60- to 80-foot (18–24 m) depth range. There are several beautiful little sandy alcoves projecting from the slope, and a number of large crevices in the 80- to 100-foot (24–30 m) zone.

Vertical Wall. About five minutes' swim to the east (right, facing seaward) of the mooring, a short vertical wall starts at a depth of around 35 feet (11 m) and ends abruptly at about 70 feet (21 m). The wall has plenty of black coral, wire corals and orange cup corals. At night, small orange ball anemones reach out from the wall into the darkness. Below the wall, the reef slope continues downward more gradually to the sand. The coral and sponges taper off at about 120 feet (36 m). The sandy slope is still fairly steep all the way down to at least 140 feet (43 m).

Since the mooring is west of the wall and the current usually heads away from the wall toward the mooring, a good profile when conditions are typical is to swim on the surface to the wall, drop as deep as you want to go, explore the wall, and then drift back toward the mooring at depth. Come up into shallow water before you get to the mooring, and do your safety stop among the fire corals and gorgonians on the shelf. When the current is running from west to east, skip the wall and enjoy the slope to the west of the mooring. It's not vertical, but it is lush.

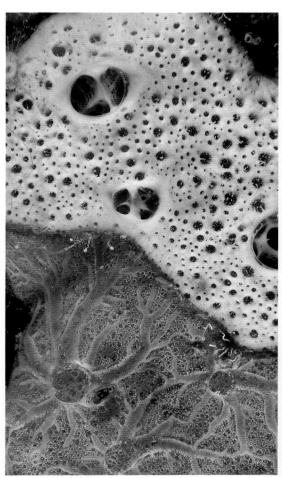

The boundary between the white and the red sponge is a slow-motion battlefield. Each sponge will try to overgrow its neighbor and occupy as much space on the reef as possible. Photo: George Lewbel.

52. JERRY'S JAM (S)

DEPTH:	20-70 FEET (6-21 M)
ACCESS:	BOAT
PARK SITE:	22

Ebo's Special, as this site is also called, has the most scenic coral and fish on the upper slope and, therefore, is a good spot for a shallow dive.

Jerry's Jam is on the north side of Klein Bonaire, just east of Carl's Hill.

The Dive. The mooring is in about 15 feet (5 m) of water on an extremely narrow shelf which has still enough unusual features to make any snorkeler happy. There is a dense thicket of fire coral, and staghorn and elkhorn coral immediately adjacent to shore where there are some beautiful small caverns. The seaward edge of the thicket looks somewhat like the rim of a castle.

The reef slope, punctuated with some very large coral heads in the upper portions, drops downward smoothly into deep water. The lower part of the reef slope has the usual stacks of plate corals, wire corals and mountainous star coral in sheets. While the lower slope is scenic, it doesn't match the upper slope with its view of the elkhorn and staghorn coral from below. Most of the good fish action tends to be near the shallows, too. At Jerry's Jam, we recommend staying above 70 feet (21 m), saving your precious deep diving time for other locations.

Photo Tip. Even if you're going deep, we recommend that photographers with wide-angle lenses save at least a few shots for the shallows. Silhouette shots will be best about mid-morning when the sun will be over Klein, directly behind the coral.

53. LEONORA'S REEF (S)

DEPTH:	30-80 FEET (9-24 M)
ACCESS:	BOAT
PARK SITE:	23

The large purple "linguini" sponge at this site is a good target for photographers.

Leonora's Reef is about half-way down the northern side of Klein Bonaire.

The Dive. The mooring is on the shallow shelf in about 10 feet (3 m) of water. There is excellent snorkeling on the shelf, which is covered with staghorn and elkhorn coral, fire coral, and yellow pencil coral. Keep an eye out for big fire worms, nudibranchs, and territorial damselfishes in the shallows.

The reef slope begins at a depth of about 30 feet (9 m). It is fairly steep, reaching near-vertical angles in the upper portions. It flattens out at depth, as the coral and sponges give way to white sand below 120 feet (36 m). There are some buttresses and parallel valleys, though they are relatively low in relief compared to some of the other Klein sites. A few low-profile terraces may be seen in the middle of the slope. There is a big purple "linguini" sponge at about 70 feet (21 m) that makes an excellent wide-angle shot. Coral and sponge cover on the slope is spotty, with some large patches of dead coral, coral rubble and sand. Below 100 feet (30 m), plate corals and flattened heads of mountainous star coral are prominent. Massive tiger groupers are particularly common at Leonora's Reef.

54. KNIFE (S)

DEPTH:	30-120 FEET (9-36 M)
ACCESS:	BOAT
PARK SITE:	24

This is a great snorkeling spot with abundant fish life.

Knife is located on the northern side of Klein Bonaire, between Sampler and Leonora's Reef.

The Dive. Its topography is similar to most of the other northern Klein sites. The mooring for Knife is at about 15 feet (5 m) near the edge of the drop-off.

Damselfishes. The moderately broad shelf is outstanding for snorkeling. Thousands of damselfishes live on the shelf and may often be seen defending their territories against foraging parrotfishes. Spanish hogfish seem particularly abundant at Knife, and are so used to divers that they may be photographed at close range, frequently eating sea urchins and scavenging in sandy spots. The shelf is covered with elkhorn, staghorn and fire coral, some of which is still recovering from storm damage.

A steep slope begins in about 30 feet (9 m) of water and drops to a sandy base below 120 feet (36 m). The slope supports large purple tube sponges, mountainous and cavernous star coral, and many other smaller species. Toward the base, larger sponges, black coral and beautiful plate corals are abundant.

Gray, French and queen angelfishes are often seen on the drop-off, and will approach divers looking for handouts. Spotted morays are also common at Knife.

Photo Tip. Photographers will get good use out of macro setups (nudibranchs abound), standard lenses for fish, or wide-angle lenses for shots of divers hanging next to the steeper portions of the upper slope.

55. SAMPLER (S)

DEPTH:	20-100 FEET (6-30 M)
ACCESS:	BOAT
PARK SITE:	25

The many ledges and alcoves found here are an ideal habitat for moray eels.

Sampler is the northernmost site on Klein, in the middle of the little "bump" on the north side of the island.

The Dive. The narrow, shallow shelf at Sampler is rather sandy, though there is some elkhorn, staghorn and fire coral. The mooring here is in about 15 feet (5 m) of water, and as at Knife and Leonora's Reef, most of the coral in shallow water is still recovering from storm damage. Snorkelers will find the fish life at Sampler particularly diverse, with many rock hinds, red hinds, coneys, parrotfishes and goatfishes in the shallows.

Green Morays and Frogfish. The reef slope begins at about 20 feet (6 m), and drops steeply downward to a sandy bottom at over 100 feet (30 m). The slope has a lot of ledges and little alcoves, many of which are inhabited by moray eels. If you're lucky, you may see one of the big green morays that were originally taught to take food from divers. People seldom hand-feed the eels nowadays due to several unpleasant incidents that we're sure you can imagine, and would rather not read about! However, the eels are still around, waiting to pose for photographers. Frogfish are also common at Sampler, though they tend to be difficult to spot while resting quietly on sponges.

These feathery animals are closely related to fire coral and are aptly named stinging hydroids. Their sting feels somewhat like an electric shock. They usually grow under overhangs and inside dark recesses in the reef. Photo: George Lewbel.

A group of small sponges next to a plate coral in deep water. Photo: George Lewbel.

56. EBO'S REEF

DEPTH:	30-80 FEET
	(9-24 M)
ACCESS:	BOAT
PARK SITE:	27

Large moray eels, groupers and filefishes are a few of the attractions on this reef.

Ebo's Reef is on the eastern side of Klein Bonaire, directly across the channel from the marina and the Sunset Beach Hotel.

The Dive. The shelf at this site is too narrow and shallow to be of much interest to snorkelers. In fact, the mooring is set on the slope about 100 feet (30 m) deep to keep boats from colliding with the shore when attached to the buoy.

The top of the slope is less than 10 feet (3 m) deep. It drops very steeply downward, with prominent buttresses and wide sand channels perpendicular to shore. The buttresses are covered with coral and orange sponges, and a great deal of black coral.

Black Coral. If you've been wondering what black coral looks like, this is your spot. Look for a dark-colored, bush-like growth with white edges, keeping in mind, of course, that collecting even a small branch may land you in jail. The buttresses extend downward to a sandy bottom at over 120 feet (36 m). Most of the good coral and black coral can be seen in the 30- to 80-foot (9-24 m) zone.

Ebo's Reef is also a good place to see large moray eels, groupers and filefishes.

THE AUTHORS' FAVORITE SITES

Southern Sites

57. RSD (RICKY-SUE-DAVE)

DEPTH:	10-130 FEET
	(3-39 M)
LEVEL:	EXPERIENCED
ACCESS:	SHORE

Enormous Nassau groupers, large sea fans, and intense fish activity in the shallow gorgonian field highlight this site.

Directions. RSD is located beyond the Salt Pier, south of town. Take the coast road past the Salt Pier, and slow down when you pass the large white house on the right before the first set of slave huts. Where the road narrows from two lanes to one, you'll see a 50 kph speed limit sign. About a sixth of a mile (1 km) south of the sign, you'll pass the first roadside turnout on the beach side of the road; park at the second. If you drive more than 1.2 miles (2 km) south of the slave huts, you've gone too far.

The Dive. The best entry and exit spot is immediately adjacent to the second turnout, where a sand channel winds between low-profile, rocky outcrops in the surf zone.

A one-minute swim over coral rubble brings you to a ragged strip of elkhorn coral parallel to the coast, about 10 feet (3 m) deep. The strip is worth a stop on the way back, if there's not too much water motion in the shallows. It has intense fish activity most of the time. It is bordered on the seaward side by another parallel sand channel that is sometimes used as a group mating area for squid during the fall.

In water from about 15 to 40 feet (5-12 m) deep on the shelf above the drop-off, there is an extremely dense gorgonian bed with sea fans up to 8 feet (2.4 m) across. At the bases of the gorgonians, look for giant Caribbean anemones with symbiotic shrimp. There are many basket stars tangled in the branches of the gorgonians. At night they open to catch plankton, expanding to the size of garbage can lids. You may also see jumbo-sized Nassau groupers, which are uncommon in other Bonaire locations.

The steep drop-off is furrowed with deep grooves perpendicular to shore, running all the way from the reef crest to the sand bottom over 150 feet (46 m) deep. Along the upper parts of the slope, you'll see black coral, huge orange sponges, purple tube sponges, lots of parrotfishes, and big brain corals. Black crinoids are abundant on top of coral heads on the middle of the slope. The lower slope is dominated by flattened stacks of plate corals, and black and yellow antipatharian sea whips (wire corals) over 10 feet (3 m) long. Schools of dolphins are sometimes seen off RSD.

Northern Sites

These sites are not recommended after rainy weather, since the mud holes get deep. Even in good weather bring fresh water to drink, and carry a tire-plugging kit and one of those adapters that lets you inflate tires with your BC hose.

58. BOCA DREIFI/CHET'S COVE

DEPTH:	15-130 FEET
	(5-39 M)
LEVEL:	EXPERIENCED
ACCESS:	SHORE

This site has large, beautiful stands of elkhorn and staghorn corals.

Directions. Drive north from Kralendijk on the paved road. Instead of turning inland toward Rincón, take the dirt road up the coast. When you get to the large oil terminal, BOPEC, don't go through the fence into the terminal. Instead turn right immediately. You'll leave the coast and head up the hill next to the storage tanks, turn left to parallel the coast, and finally return to the coast on the other side. About 1.2 miles (2 km) farther north, you'll see some large radio antennas and a couple of buildings on your left labeled, "Geowatt Research Center." The dive site is the cove to the north of the buildings. Park to the right of the buildings near the natural stone steps leading down into the left side of the cove and ask for permission at the house.

The Dive. Chet's Cove (Boca Dreifi on maps) has a nice little sandy beach for gearing up, and a well-protected entry and exit. Toward the left side of the cove, a narrow channel runs from shore out through an elkhorn coral bed. The outer end of the channel is difficult to spot from sea so it's best to drop a small temporary marker buoy to facilitate your return.

The shelf has very heavy coral cover, with beautiful large staghorn and elkhorn thickets in shallow water. Juvenile spotted drums and other young fishes are abundant in the protective matrix formed by these thickets. Schools of goatfish are usually at work in the sandier portions. Bluish-colored lettuce slugs

are extremely abundant on the staghorn coral.

The reef slope begins in about 40 feet (12 m) of water, and drops sharply downward. The coral gradually changes from star corals to plate corals and wire corals, and eventually to sand. Keep an eye seaward as a school of hammerheads has been spotted here.

59. PLAYA FRANS

DEPTH:	15-130 FEET
	(5-39 M)
LEVEL:	EXPERIENCED
ACCESS:	SHORE

Massive star coral heads that look like they've never seen a fin characterize the slope.

Directions. Continue a few kilometers north of Chet's Cove until the road dead-ends at a fishing camp. Skiffs are often pulled up on the beach. Smile and wave, but stay out of the way of the locals working there—they're not on vacation like you are—and be careful of lines and hooks that may be lying around, above or below the waterline.

The Dive. The easiest entry is from the sandy beach in front of the garage-like building that houses several fishing boats. There is quite a bit of elkhorn coral in shallow water, but temporary fishing buoys usually are there to mark a channel through the coral. If the buoys are in place, you can use them to navigate across the shelf. The channel leads out and slightly to the left of the center of the garage. The shelf itself is fairly uninteresting, and littered with tires, lines, old anchors, and other debris. Nonetheless, a lot of small fishes linger here, probably feeding on the remains of their unfortunate larger fellows who get gutted and cleaned there by fishermen. Farther out, tarpon will most likely cruise by you for a closer look, and you may see conchs and other large snails crawling around on the sand.

The slope starts at about 40 feet (12 m), falls off at about 45°, and is covered with perfect coral heads. The terrain is irregular. Massive star coral heads stair-step down into water over 130 feet (39 m) deep. Remember to look offshore; hammerheads and a manta ray have been sighted here by the authors' buddies.

CHAPTER **VI**   MARINE LIFE

When divers drop in on their first coral reef, they are always amazed—and often overwhelmed—by the sheer complexity of the underwater scenery facing them. Thousands of brightly colored fishes swirl around a mosaic of alien-looking patches that cover the reef. After a dive or two, those patches and fishes start to fit into recognizable groups such as sponges and corals, and parrotfishes and angelfishes. The learning process continues, dive after dive, until seasoned veterans can find old friends and familiar species on any reef.

Providing a photographic catalog or a complete listing of all these fishes and invertebrates is far beyond the scope of this book. Several hundred species can be observed in the scuba zone during the daytime. By searching carefully for cryptic species that hide in crevices or are out only at night you can see nearly double that number.

We have included here those species most likely to be seen by an alert diver during a typical week of diving. To make the best use of this chapter we strongly recommend that you read it in conjunction with an identification book on fishes and invertebrates.

fistularis), and the bluish-pink **fluorescent sponge** (*Callyspongia plicifera*). They are found on reefs all over the Caribbean. Other less visible—but even more abundant—sponges are the boring sponges, various species of the genus *Cliona*. They live in cracks and holes in coral. Boring sponges dissolve the calcium carbonate skeleton of corals, eventually eroding coral heads from the inside and causing them to crumble.

Sponges are filter-feeders, pumping seawater through tiny pores all over their outsides. The water travels through internal canals to microscopic chambers where oxygen and fine particles of food are removed, and carbon dioxide and metabolic wastes, such as ammonia, are dumped. The water is then pumped back outside.

Sponges are extraordinarily efficient filters, removing particles below 1/25,000 of an inch (0.001 mm) in size. They can pump very large volumes of water, given enough time. For example, a grapefruit-size sponge can filter about 400 gallons (1500 L) of water in 24 hours!

Invertebrates

SPONGES

Sponges are permanently attached animals belonging to the phylum Porifera, meaning ''hole bearing.'' Some common sponges are large and conspicuous, such as the hard, gray **barrel sponge** (*Xestospongia muta*); the bright yellow-green **candle sponge** (*Verongia*

The brown carpet or stinging anemone usually nestles in crevices, and can be recognized by its fringed tentacles with whitish bulbs. Unlike nearly all other Caribbean anemones, this one can do you some harm. Its stinging cells can raise a red welt on your skin within minutes of contact. Photo: George Lewbel.

Thousands of tiny anemones share the porous surface of the sponge beneath them with a small brittle star. This surface amounts to a coarse intake filter. Water rich in organic nutrients and oxygen enters the sponge through the surface. Oxygen and nutrients are extracted, carbon dioxide and organic wastes are added, and the waste water is then pumped back out through the larger holes. The sponge's complex inner structure can be seen through the two visible exhaust ports.
Photo: Larry Martin.

SYMBIOSIS: ANEMONES AND SPONGES

Although most anemones are solitary, there are some very interesting colonial anemones that live in sponges. Next time you see a sponge that appears to be covered with tiny white or yellow dots, take a closer look. Each of the dots is a little zoanthid anemone. Chemical extracts of zoanthid anemones are poisonous to some species of fish, and the combination of sponge spicules and anemones is probably a difficult meal to digest! This may be one reason that you rarely see sponges with bites taken out of them.

ANEMONES, CORALS, AND RELATIVES

Anemones (pronounced "un-nem-oh-knees"), corals, gorgonians and jellyfish are all in the phylum Cnidaria, the name derived from the Greek *cnidos*, or thread. All cnidarians have thread-like microscopic structures in their tissues. These structures include tangling, adhesive loops that snare prey, and hollow hypodermic tubes that pump stinging, toxic chemicals into animals that touch them. The stinging threads are called nematocysts, and are fired upon physical contact. Most nematocysts are harmless to humans, but there are a few exceptions.

Cnidarians have soft, hollow bodies with a centrally located mouth surrounded by tentacles. Most of the nematocysts are on the tentacles. Whatever they capture with their nematocysts is inserted by the tentacles into the mouth. The prey is then digested inside the hollow body, and non-digestible parts (bones, shells) are dumped back out the mouth. Cnidarians also have nervous systems with sensors that respond to light, touch and taste, and some of them have pretty good eyes too.

Anemones

Anemones are usually stuck to the reef, but they can and do occasionally move about. Most anemones have nematocysts that cannot penetrate the thick skin of the palms of your hands or your fingertips. Generally, anemones will retract their tentacles if touched, so photographers will want to keep their framers from touching the tentacles.

The most conspicuous large anemone is the **giant Caribbean anemone** (*Condylactis gigantea*). It comes in a variety of colors, including purple, pink, green and yellow, and has low-powered nematocysts that won't sting your fingers. It has fat tentacles with bulbous tips, and grows to a diameter of about a foot.

If you look in empty conch shells or at the base of coral heads, you will eventually see the **ringed anemone** (*Bartholomea annulata*), which has thin, pointed, clear tentacles ringed with white spiral bands. The bands bear the nematocysts. The ringed anemone almost always has one or two pistol shrimps living among its tentacles. If you try to touch one of them, they will snap their claws loudly and probably make you jump.

You may also see the **Caribbean mist anemone** (*Heteractis lucida*), an animal with thin, transparent tentacles covered with tiny white balls that look like a cloud of mist. The balls are batteries of nematocysts.

There are at least two large Caribbean anemones capable of stinging you vigorously. One is the **sun anemone** (*Stoichactis helianthis*). It has short, stubby tentacles all over its face, and gets up to a foot across. It's usually pale green or yellow and found in shallow water, near the shoreward side of reefs or in areas with freshwater runoff. The other is the **stinging anemone** (*Lebrunea danae*). It usually has soft, brown, highly branched tentacles which protrude from between coral heads and stick out of crevices. It looks like the fringe of a rug.

Corals

Corals are colonies of interconnected animals (polyps) similar in structure to anemones. Individual coral animals have mouths and tentacles with nematocysts, and feed as anemones do. They are genetically identical to one another within colonies, since members of each colony occasionally divide in half or bud off to produce new members on the edges of the colony.

Corals are dependent upon microscopic internal plants (zooxanthellae) which supply organic compounds and aid the corals to crystallize calcium carbonate, from which they make their hard skeletons. It is the chlorophyll and the pigments in zooxanthellae that give corals their color.

Each species of coral has a distinctive type of skeleton, and every coral colony has its own shape, influenced by the environment in which it grows. That's why no two reefs are identical. When many colonies grow near one another, their skeletons may become fused into a single mass which we call a reef.

In shallow water, the most common corals are often the **staghorn** (*Acropora cervicornis*) and **elkhorn** (*Acropora palmata*). Elkhorn seems to be particularly good at withstanding and recovering from wave damage. Staghorn has one of the fastest growth rates among the corals (still less than one foot per year), and can form huge thickets, usually a bit deeper than elkhorn coral.

Below the zone of elkhorn and staghorn, there is usually a mixture of corals. In relatively protected areas and on shallow patch reefs, various **leaf** and **ribbon corals** of the genus *Agaricia* often predominate. They are thin and somewhat fragile, and most of them prefer quiet waters. Their close relatives, the **plate corals**, are even more fragile, and form big sheets in deeper water or under overhangs and in caverns.

Farther down the slope, most large reef complexes are dominated by the **mountainous star coral** (*Montastrea annularis*), and its relative (*Montastrea cavernosa*), the **cavernous star coral**. The star corals are the main reef builders in most

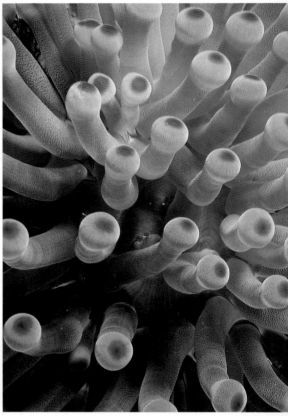

Giant Caribbean anemones can dissolve living coral polyps around them, thereby creating a light-colored "halo" of dead coral. In this way, they guarantee that their dwellings will not be altered or eliminated by further coral growth. They come in a wide variety of colors, and harbor several kinds of symbiotic shrimp and fishes. These are the only anemones in the scuba zone with large, finger-sized unbranched tentacles. Stinging cells make giant Caribbean anemones feel sticky to the touch, but they cannot harm you. Photos: George Lewbel.

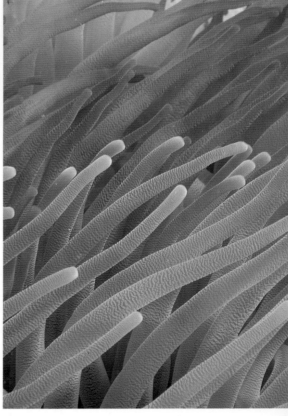

areas of the Caribbean. Both of these star corals can form huge mounds or heads in shallower depths, or big flattened plates in deeper water. Buttresses are often formed by star corals, and as you swim downward along their faces, you can see the star coral change gradually from mounds to plates with increasing depth.

The same species can have different growth forms at different depths because of a tradeoff between the need for light and the need for physical strength to resist erosion and wave action. Corals need sunlight for photosynthesis by their internal plants. At shallower depths where light is abundant but wave action is stronger, corals will be compact. At depth, corals form plates to increase their surface area to collect more light. These plates are more fragile, but at depth there is no wave action to damage them.

Rounded, massive corals are abundant on Caribbean reefs. The most common species are the **giant brain coral** (*Colpophyllia natans*), and three species of the genus *Diploria*: the **grooved brain coral** (*Diploria labyrinthiformis*), the **smooth brain coral** (*Diploria strigosa*), and the **knobby brain coral** (*Diploria clivosa*).

The **rough** and **smooth starlet corals** (*Siderastrea radians* and *Siderastrea siderea*) form basketball-sized round heads here and there. Brain and starlet corals grow very slowly—often much less than an inch (2.5 cm) per year—but they're very sturdy and their rounded shape gives them tremendous resistance to wave shock. It wouldn't be out of the ordinary to find a brain coral a century old.

One of the showiest corals is *Dendrogyra cylindricus*, the **pillar coral**, which forms spectacular white colonies up to ten feet high. Pillar corals usually have their tentacles out during the day, giving them a fuzzy appearance. If disturbed, they will retract in waves passing over the surface of the coral.

There are some very interesting, less conspicuous corals on Caribbean reefs. The **fungus corals** (various species of the genus *Mycetophyllia*) are easy to find. They grow beautiful, brightly colored plates that look like pizzas on steep surfaces, usually fairly deep.

Down in cubbyholes, you may spot something that looks like a glowing green donut or flying saucer. It's either *Scolymia lacera* or *Scolymia cubensis*, the solitary **disk corals**. They have nematocysts that can zap their fellow corals, and specialize in dissolving their neighbors to clear space around them. They are also fluorescent. That yellowish-green color is due to the absorption of blue light and its re-emission at longer wavelengths.

In the sand channels between patch reefs, you may come across the **rose coral** (*Manicina areolata*), a free-living Caribbean coral that can crawl around! It starts out life attached, but later breaks off and goes it alone. It looks like a brownish mouth up to about six inches long, resting on the surface of the sand. You'll probably also see the skeletons of dead ones looking like smiling white mouths grinning up at you from the sand.

An archway formed by erosion in a mountainous star coral head. Erosion usually begins with mechanical damage, followed by invasion of the coral skeleton by boring sponges and clams. Photo: George Lewbel.

Fire Coral

There are at least three common species (or growth forms) of fire coral in the Caribbean: *Millepora squarrosa*, *Millepora alcicornis* and *Millepora complanata*. Fire coral can grow on its own as flat sheets or boxlike formations, or encrust gorgonians, coral heads, or even concrete surfaces. Strictly speaking, it isn't coral—it's more closely related to the Portuguese man-of-war. Fire coral has nematocysts that cause immediate stinging, and can produce dermatitis on sensitive skin. If you don't touch anything that looks like dull tan paint, you'll avoid most fire coral.

Stinging Hydroids

Closely related to fire coral are the stinging hydroids, a group of similar species that form lacy black fan-like colonies. Stinging hydroids usually grow under overhangs and in caverns. They have high-powered nematocysts whose sting is sometimes described as "electric."

Fire coral colonies have a number of growth forms, though they are all tan-colored with white edges. Sometimes they spread out on non-living objects such as gorgonian skeletons, mooring lines, or buoys. They also form erect branching or plate-like colonies. They are more closely related to the Portuguese man-of-war than to other hard corals. Photos: George Lewbel.

Portuguese Man-of-War

The Portuguese man-of-war (*Physalia* species) is not a true jellyfish, being related more closely to fire corals and stinging hydroids. The man-of-war has a gas-filled sac that floats on the surface. The float is up to eight inches (20 cm) long, and has a little sail which causes the man-of-war to travel with the wind. There are even right- and left-handed men-of-war; the angle of the sail causes some to move consistently about 45 degrees to the right side of the direction of the wind, and others to the left. Every man-of-war has long, trailing tentacles hanging below it. These tentacles are covered with nematocysts that are capable of catching fish, and inflicting a painful sting in humans. If you see them, stay well clear; the tentacles can be extremely long.

Gorgonians

Gorgonians include the sea fans, sea rods and sea fingers. They, too, are colonial cnidarians.

Gorgonians have flexible skeletons made of protein and calcium carbonate spicules. Some species have internal plants (as do corals). The more spicules, and the more closely they are fused to one another, the harder the skeleton.

Perhaps the most interesting gorgonians from a diver's standpoint are the **common sea fan** (*Gorgonia ventalina*), and the **Venus sea fan** (*Gorgonia flabellum*). These flat-bladed yellow and purple colonies are about three feet (1 m) high, and can serve as navigational aids underwater since they face 90 degrees to the average direction of water motion.

Black Coral

Black corals are colonial cnidarians not closely related to gorgonians, but very similar in appearance. Many Caribbean governments have banned the collection of black corals. Where not legally protected, they are becoming very scarce. Gorgonians and black coral grow very slowly. If you take or break a colony, you can destroy years (if not decades) of growth in a few thoughtless seconds. By the way, on some islands, you'll go to jail if you are caught taking black coral.

"HAZARDOUS" MARINE LIFE: COMMON SENSE

Bonaire's marine life is almost entirely benign, but careless diving techniques can introduce you to the marvelous defensive mechanisms some animals have. Sea urchin spines can penetrate boots, gloves and wet suits; coral can cut you; fire coral can sting you; sponges can produce impressive rashes; stingrays and scorpionfish can stick a poisonous spine into you if molested; and moray eels do occasionally bite if tempted by food or harassed for photos.

To stay in one piece, simply keep your eyes open and your hands to yourself. At night, sea wasps may produce severe stings. To reduce your chances of getting zapped on a night dive, cover up. Wear a full wet suit or diveskin including a hood, gloves and boots. Avoid lingering in shallow water. Sea wasps tend to be near the surface after dark, and often cluster near lights.

Jellyfish

Jellyfish are cnidarians that swim through the water and have hollow bodies with a single, central mouth facing downward. Their nematocysts are borne on tentacles and mouthparts that hang down from the main part of the body. The body pulsates rhythmically to propel the jellyfish through the water in search of fish and plankton.

Despite their blobby appearance, jellyfish deserve more respect than they usually get, not only for their ability to sting you thoroughly with their nematocysts. They're more complicated than they look. At the base of their tentacles are gravity receptors that keep them right-side-up, and light detectors. Sea wasps even have eyes with corneas, lenses, and complex retinas which can probably form pretty detailed images.

The most common large jellyfish seen above coral reefs is the **moon jelly** (*Aurita aurita*). It's usually less than two feet (61 cm) in diameter, with small tentacles around the rim and a large, dangling set of mouthparts. It is a slow swimmer and fairly easy to avoid, though its tentacles are transparent and easy to bump into if you swim too close to the bell.

Sea wasps are small, clear jellyfish seen near the surface, mainly at night. They spend the day in deep water, but rise at dusk to feed in shallow water. They have squarish transparent bodies, are usually from two to six inches (5–15 cm) long, and trail one or more tentacles from each lower corner of the body. The nematocysts on those tentacles can cause severe reactions, including local tissue destruction, extreme pain and even respiratory difficulties.

Corallimorpharians

Corallimorpharians are small but astonishingly sensual cnidarians overlooked by most divers. Closely related to both corals and anemones, the most abundant species, *Ricordea florida* and *Rhodactis sanctihomae*, look like mashed or flattened greenish-brown anemones two to three inches (5–7cm) across and only a quarter to a half inch (6–13 mm) high. They often grow in colonies, forming sheets on vertical surfaces. You'll see a tiny nipple-like mouth in the center of each individual, and tiny bumps or tentacles on its "face." Touch it gently with a bare finger; you'll like the way it feels.

A less common corallimorpharian is known as the **orange ball anemone**. Seen only at night, it is highly sensitive and retracts quickly if you shine a light on it. It looks like a small, transparent column up to about six inches (15 cm) long and one inch (2.5 cm) in diameter. Its tentacles are transparent, and have fluorescent orange balls on their tips! You can usually find them in nooks and crannies that don't have much light in the daytime, although they won't open until dark.

Segmented Worms

Our non-diving friends often roll their eyes around when we extoll the beauty of marine worms of the phylum Annelida. That's because they haven't seen them, and wouldn't recognize them if they had. The worms that most divers see on Caribbean coral reefs are feather duster worms, Christmas tree worms and fire worms. These animals have long, segmented bodies, divided into sections like a train. They are much more complicated in structure than the cnidarians. They have longitudinal nerve cords; circulatory systems with blood; primitive kidneys; muscles; and intestines, with a mouth at one end and an anus at the other, unlike the cnidarians which have but one opening to eat and excrete through.

Feather duster worms (*Sabellastarte magnifica*) live in a soft, membranous tube. They never leave their tubes. Their spectacular, fluffy brown and white plumes grow up to four inches (10 cm) across, and are combined respiratory and feeding structures. The worms pump blood through their plumes to take up oxygen and release carbon dioxide, and catch plankton and tiny food particles from the water on the plume. If you startle feather dusters, they will pull back into their tubes faster than the eye can follow. Both the Christmas tree worm and the feather duster worm have light-sensitive eyes just below the plumes, and the mere shadow of a diver's hand is enough to make them retract rapidly.

Christmas tree worms (*Spirobranchus giganteus*) live in a hard tube of calcium carbonate. Christmas tree worms come in a variety of colors, including white, yellow, brown and red. Their two spiraled plumes serve the same functions as the plume in the feather duster: feeding and respiration. Christmas tree worms can plug the opening to their tubes when disturbed. After they pull in their plume, they fill the hole with a hatch cover attached to the outermost part of their bodies. These covers are the purple and white structures you can see between the spirals.

Hermodice carunculata, the **fire worm**, looks like a red and white centipede, and should be treated with similar respect. Along its side are thousands of tiny white bristles. When the fire worm is disturbed, it flares them out in a threat display. If you ignore the threat and touch a fire worm, these bristles will be embedded in your skin, producing immediate pain and irritation. Fire worms eat living coral and breed in huge piles, pouring clouds of eggs and sperm into the water around them.

SEA STARS, URCHINS, AND RELATIVES

The word "echinoderm" means spiny skin. The echinoderms include some of our favorite Caribbean animals, such as sea stars, and some of our least favorite animals, such as sea urchins. Most echinoderms have five similar sections radiating out from their centers, like the segments of an orange. Echinoderms have hard internal parts made primarily of calcium carbonate. In echinoderms such as sea cucumbers, these pieces are not connected to one another, allowing the animals a great deal of flexibility. In other groups such as the urchins, the pieces are fused together for strength, forming a rigid sphere.

Perhaps the most striking anatomical feature of the echinoderms is their hydraulic system. Many of them, such as sea stars and urchins, have tiny tubular feet between their spines. These tube feet can be extended by changes in water pressure within them. The animal takes water in through a filtering screen and pumps it through internal channels to wherever it's needed for locomotion. The hydraulic system is supplemented by muscles,

Fire worms or bristle worms come in two varieties: red with poisonous white bristles, and greenish with poisonous white bristles. The bristles sting immediately, and will stick to your gloves or wet suit. This can result in a delayed encounter of the worst kind when you remove your dive gear. Photo: George Lewbel.

used by urchins to rotate their spines, by cucumbers to pull back into their holes, and by brittle stars to move their legs.

Sea Stars

The most commonly seen sea stars in the Caribbean are **reticulated sea stars** (*Oreaster reticulatus*). They usually have five arms, but sometimes have as many as seven or as few as four, and a net-like pattern on the upper surface. They range in color from red to green, though orange ones are most often seen. They get up to a foot (30 cm) across and six inches (15 cm) high.

If you're looking in the sand, you may also see the **Caribbean sand star** (*Astropecten duplicatus*). The sand star has five long, pointed arms and a set of plates that look like Chiclets along the outer edges of each arm. It's usually about the size of your hand.

Sea Urchins

There are many kinds of sea urchins in the Caribbean. For example, *Eucidaris tribuloides*, the **pencil urchin**, has thick, blunt spines frequently used for wind chimes and jewelry. *Tripneustes ventricosus*, the **West Indian sea egg**, has a black body and very short white spines, and can be touched bare-handed; its eggs are often eaten by locals. *Meoma ventricosa*, the **West Indian sea biscuit**, is a fat reddish-brown urchin about the size and shape of a flattened grapefruit, with five radial grooves on its top, and stiff little spines all over the body. It is usually seen out on the sand by night divers. It hides just under the sand during the daytime, but emerges to graze at night.

The single animal feared the most by Caribbean divers is the **long-spined sea urchin** (*Diadema antillarum*). It comes in basic black, as well as white, and black-and-white varieties, and gets as large as a basketball in some places. *Diadema antillarum* rests quietly during the day under ledges and in holes, and comes out at night to graze.

The long-spined sea urchin has good light sensors, and can detect fish or divers swimming overhead. When it does, it swings its spines into position, pointing directly at the possible threat. The urchins have enemies, such as triggerfishes and Spanish hogfish, that try to turn it over so the spines aren't in the way, and then eat it.

Sea Cucumbers

There are a number of large sea cucumber species in the Caribbean. Divers usually see two of them frequently. The brown **lion's paw sea cucumber** (*Holothuria thomasi*) grows up to six feet (2 m) long and lives in holes. It is rarely seen in the daytime. At night, it reaches out sucking up organic matter from the bottom around its coral head. The **donkey dung sea cucumber** (*Holothuria mexicana*)—yes, it's actually called that in the scientific literature—has a thick, brown or gray leathery skin. Its undersurface is flattened and rose-colored, and has tiny tube feet on it. It crawls about freely but very slowly. Not being as soft and vulnerable as the lion's paw, it

doesn't need a permanent hideout. It doesn't seem to mind being handled gently.

Brittle Stars and Basket Stars

Brittle stars and basket stars are echinoderms that have long, skinny arms used to catch particles drifting in the water. Brittle stars are often seen on the outside of sponges, looking like spiders. They take advantage of the feeding currents that the sponges produce. One of the most common, *Ophiothrix suensonii*, the **sponge brittle star**, is usually draped all over purple vase sponges. It has a small, soft disk in its center, and five very thin, hairy-looking arms.

Basket stars have five arms also, but they are highly branched, making them look like huge birds' nests. The **Caribbean basket star** (*Astrophyton muricatum*), gets up to three feet (1 m) in diameter when fully expanded at night. During the daytime, basket stars roll up all their arms and look like little balls the size of your fist. You can often find them tightly wrapped around gorgonian branches.

Crinoids

Those fluffy-looking, long orange branches that stick out of cracks in reefs and are curled like a fiddle head at the tip are the arms of the **orange crinoid** (*Nemaster rubignosa*). The arms feel sticky because they are used to catch plankton. The **black-and-white crinoid** (*Nemaster grandis*), actually crawls around. It can be seen perched on top of sponges and coral heads, looking like a stiff bouquet of black feathers with white tips, almost a foot (30 cm) high.

West Indian sea eggs are large black urchins with short white spines. Sea eggs temporarily attach bits of plant matter and shells to themselves. The debris may serve as camouflage, or perhaps protects them from bright sunlight. They live in shallow water up on the shelf. Their ripe gonads are eaten by the locals on many islands. Photo: George Lewbel.

CRUSTACEANS

Crustaceans include groups such as barnacles, shrimps, crabs and lobsters. The crustaceans have jointed legs and a hard outer covering called an exoskeleton that is periodically shed. They reproduce sexually, and many of them have internal fertilization followed by external brooding of eggs. Their eyes are typically excellent, as any diver who has tried to sneak up on a lobster in the daytime knows.

Spider Crabs

The largest crab you will find is the **reef spider crab** (*Mithrax spinosissimus*). This reddish-brown, fuzzy crab has long legs and a body that can get almost as large as a volleyball. You won't see it in the daytime except in caves and under overhangs. It is

usually out at night looking for plants to eat. It cannot be mistaken for any other crab on Caribbean reefs; it is similar in shape (and is closely related) to Alaskan king crabs whose legs are so popular in restaurants.

Coral Crabs

Another common large crab out mainly at night is the **coral crab** (*Carpilius corallinus*). It has a bright red, smooth body with fine lines and spots on top. The tips of its claws are darker colored, or sometimes purple. It reaches the size of a hubcap, and is faster than it looks.

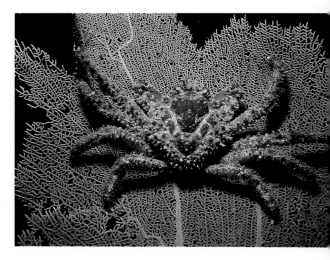

Crustaceans come out of their hiding places on the reef to feed at night. This red crab has climbed up on a gorgonian sea fan. Photo: George Lewbel.

Arrow Crabs

Arrow crabs (*Stenorhynchus seticornis*) look like big spiders, with spindly legs up to about four inches (10 cm) long and little bodies the size of a dime with a long, spear-like rostrum (spike on the head) that sticks out between two beady, stalked eyes. Arrow crabs are tan with brown and white stripes, and there are two little purple claws on the front legs. You'll see them most often hiking around on sponges.

Cleaner Shrimps

The cleaner shrimps are those crustaceans that live on or near other, larger animals, and make their living picking up scraps or eating parasites. There are many species of cleaner shrimps associated with anemones, for example. They utilize the protection offered by the anemones against larger predators, and are immune themselves to the anemones' nematocysts. They clean parasites from fish that stop nearby. Other cleaners live on sponges or in crevices. Some of the more common small cleaners—usually less than an inch (2.5 cm) long—include **Pederson's cleaning shrimp** (*Periclimenes pedersoni*),

FIRST AID FOR CUTS AND STINGS

Sponge Rash. Many species of sponges have microscopic spicules that can easily penetrate your skin or stick in your wet suit and gloves. You'll find them when you unsuit and touch bare skin. Also, some chemicals secreted by sponges are highly irritating to humans.

If you get spicules in your skin, they will cause mild to severe itching and dermatitis. We've tried to remove them with sticky tape, but scraping them off on a sharp edge seems to do as much or as little good. Some people advocate rinsing with vinegar, mild ammonia or meat tenderizer. Once in a while, these remedies seem to reduce chemical irritation. You usually have to live with the spicules until they drop out after a couple of days. Cortisone cream often helps. If the itching gets worse, see a doctor.

Coral Cuts. If you bang into corals, their skeletons will cut you, and the cuts often infect, especially if you stay wet. For shallow cuts and abrasions, clean the scrape with soap and water followed by a mild antiseptic such as hydrogen peroxide, and then cover the wound with Neosporin ointment and a bandage. Get a doctor to clean out any deep cuts or deal with infections, and keep your tetanus shots current.

Cnidarian Stings. Small stings, such as those from fire coral, usually just hurt for an hour or so and go away on their own. Some divers claim that meat tenderizer can detoxify the venom and reduce the pain. We've had minimal luck with it. We have had relief with cortisone cream on mild stings, but we've never tried it on a severe sting.

Pistol Shrimps

transparent with purple and white stripes, and often found on the anemones described above; and the **red-backed cleaning shrimp** (*Lysmata grabhami*), clear with a wide red band down its back and a thin white stripe down the middle of the band. Both of these species will try to clean your hand if you hold it still near them.

The largest cleaner is the **red-banded coral shrimp** (*Stenopus hispidus*), which looks like a little mini-lobster with its long claws and red-and-white banded body. Its very long, white antennae will tip you off to its presence in crevices.

The pistol shrimps, which are also called snapping shrimps, are usually heard but not seen. They are generally less than an inch (2.5 cm) long, and hide deep in holes or beneath anemones. If you pause momentarily between inhalation and exhalation while sitting on the bottom near a coral reef in calm seas, you may hear a series of little snaps or pops. These sounds are generated by members of the genus *Alpheus*, the pistol shrimps. They make the snap by cocking one tiny claw like the hammer on a pistol, then holding it in place with an internal locking mechanism while muscles that normally close the claw are tightened. When the muscles are

---

If you get stung by a jellyfish or man-of-war, bits of tentacle may stick to your skin. Some of the nematocysts in these tentacles will have already fired, while others are still waiting their turn. If possible, try to avoid firing the nematocysts on any tentacles adhering to your skin. If you can lift the tentacles off gently and carefully with gloves, you'll minimize the damage. Don't try to rub the tentacles off with sand; you'll just fire everything that's left into your skin.

If you get badly stung by any cnidarian, you may need medical assistance, especially if you're prone to allergic reactions.

Urchin Wounds. The sea urchin's spines are sharper than needles, and will easily penetrate a wet suit. If you do get stuck, expect some immediate pain. The spines are barbed, and usually break off in the wound. We've tried to dig them out, but it is generally impossible.

Some advocate soaking the wound in vinegar to dissolve the spine, while others just leave it alone. The spine will usually dissolve in the body and/or fester and be rejected, but it takes a couple of weeks. It's another good reason to have a current tetanus shot before you go diving. There is a mild toxin in the spines so if you're prone to allergic reactions, or if the wound is deep or infects and the pain persists, you should see a doctor. You can't really do much of a job disinfecting urchin punctures yourself, though we always rub Neosporin on the wound to convince our aching body that we've done something useful. We guarantee that after you get stuck, you'll be more careful next time.

maximally contracted, the shrimp releases the lock and the claw slams shut. It's such a powerful snap that it can stun small fishes that the shrimps then eat!

Red Coral Shrimps

If you're out at night over a coral reef, you'll undoubtedly see thousands of glowing red eyes reflecting the light of your dive light back at you. These eyes belong to **red coral shrimps** (*Rhynchocinetes rigens*), which grow to about four inches (10 cm) long, and which are out only at night.

Slipper Lobsters

There are a number of Caribbean species of slipper lobsters; most are members of the genus *Scyllarides*. They have no claws or long antennae, and are flattened in appearance. They get up to a foot (30 cm) long, but most are smaller. Like the spiny lobsters, they hide in the daytime but come out at night to feed. If you find something that's not quite a crab or a lobster, and is tan or brown, it's probably a slipper lobster.

Spiny Lobsters

There are two different species of spiny lobsters on Caribbean reefs: the **common spiny lobster** (*Panulirus argus*) and the **spotted spiny lobster** (*Panulirus guttatus*). They are easy to tell apart: the common spiny lobster has a light tan or orange body, while the spotted spiny lobster has a very dark colored body with light colored spots on it. Both of them spend their daytimes nestled under coral heads and in caves, and come out at night. Neither of them has claws, but the long antennae, body and tail are covered with sharp spines to protect them against predators, and the two sharp "horns" above the eyes can draw blood from a careless diver. They can also make a startling noise that sounds like rubbing a violin string with rosin; the noise is made by scraping their antennae against ridges on their exoskeletons.

Molluscs

Molluscs are snails, clams, squids, octopuses, and their relatives. When shell collectors were limited to whatever washed up on beaches, their impact on marine life was minimal. However, since divers can easily get at many previously rare shells, some species have been driven nearly to extinction in a few decades. Bonaire's regulations do not permit you to take living shells, so bring home a photograph instead, and leave the animal alive and well on the bottom.

Chitons

Everyone who dives from ironshore will wonder sooner or later what those little one inch (2.5 cm) long oval depressions are next to the water, and what those little creatures that look like pill bugs in each depression might be. Those creatures are chitons and they are among the oldest and most primitive of molluscs. Chitons have eight overlapping calcium carbonate plates on their backs, making them look a bit like pill bugs, and a fuzzy band around their outer edges.

They leave their spots at high tide to graze, and return to nestle down into the same location. Over a period of years, they grow and gradually enlarge their depressions.

Conchs

Conchs are large snails that crawl slowly along in sandy areas, especially in seagrass beds. The conch taken most often for food, and the one that divers in the Caribbean are most likely to see, is the **queen conch** (*Strombus gigas*), which has a whitish-pink shell that is bright pink on the bottom, and grows up to a foot (30 cm) long.

Flamingo Tongues

The **flamingo tongue** (*Cyphoma gibbosum*) is a small, yellowish snail with beautiful dark colored spots. If it is disturbed, it slowly retracts its spotted mantle, revealing a smooth pink shell. Flamingo tongues live on gorgonians, eating their living tissues and leaving bare patches on their hosts.

This nudibranch, which is sometimes called a lettuce slug, is common in shallow water, especially on branches of staghorn coral. It and most of its close relatives are poisonous to fish. The lettuce slug looks greenish because chlorophyll-bearing structures (chloroplasts) in its diet have been moved to its dorsal gills. Photo: George Lewbel.

All of these snails have gathered to breed at the same time. Such reproductive aggregations are not unusual for marine animals, and very common for molluscs. Photo: George Lewbel.

Nudibranchs

Nudibranchs are closely related to snails, but have no shell. They carry their gills exposed on their backs—hence the name "nudibranch," which means "naked gill." Nudibranchs seem to be highly repellent and/or poisonous, and are rarely bothered by other marine animals. In fact, a number of nudibranchs actually eat cnidarians, but somehow keep their nematocysts from firing during the digestive process. These unfired nematocysts are then transferred by the nudibranchs to their gills, where they provide additional protection.

There are several common nudibranchs on Caribbean coral reefs, but the one that is easiest to find is the **lettuce slug** (*Tridachia crispata*). The lettuce slug is usually about 2 inches (5 cm) long, pale green or blue, and has fluffy white gills all over its back. Next time you're near shore at the end of the dive, look around the staghorn coral, where they are most abundant.

Squids

The only squid that divers are likely to see on Caribbean coral reefs is the **reef squid** (*Sepioteuthis sepioidea*). It's a small squid, generally less than a foot (30 cm) long, with a fat little body and ten short arms. It is common to find them in groups of three or four swimming together, changing colors rapidly from white to green to brown.

Don't bother to try to sneak up on them; their eyes are probably just about as good as yours and they can swim faster than you can. Just swim slowly along, edging near them, and hope that they're feeling friendly.

Octopuses

Octopuses are the undercover camouflage champions of the reef. They crawl along the bottom, changing their colors and patterns to match their surroundings. They can go from near black to white and back as fast as you can blink, and can reproduce the appearance of cobbles, sand, and almost anything they're near. They are active predators, seeking out fishes, lobsters, crabs and other large prey at night, and hiding during the daytime. When they catch something with their eight sucker-bearing arms, they can bite it with a beak that lies in the center of the arms on the underside. The most common octopus that divers see is *Octopus briareus*, the **reef octopus**. You're most likely to see them at night when they're out hunting.

The beak of an octopus can inject venom. Caribbean species don't often bite humans, and their bite is not known to be especially dangerous, but it can cause a whopping infection. If you get bitten by an octopus, you should see a doctor.

This young French angelfish is losing its juvenile bars and gaining the yellow-rimmed scales that differentiate adult French angels from their more drab cousins, the gray angelfish. Photo: George Lewbel.

You're not very likely to spot octopuses during the daytime when they hide deep in the reef. At night, they're out hunting. Photo: George Lewbel.

PINK FLAMINGO: CHOGOGO

Bonaire is one of the few nesting places in the world for the pink flamingo. The Pekelmeer colony, a sanctuary set up by the Antillean International Salt Company, can have as many as 4,000 nesting pairs. Flamingos are very shy and tourists should be extremely cautious when approaching them, especially during the nesting season. Disturbance can cause panic, creating broken eggs and wings, and trampled nests. An air show in 1944 caused the flamingos to leave Bonaire for six years.

Flamingos make a high nasal honking noise which sounds like "chogogo," which is what the Bonaireans call them. They feed on brine fly pupae, brine shrimp, algae and organic material filtered from the bottom sediment. They also eat the tiny clams and snails found in the lagoons. Flamingos are not born pink. Natural substances in their food source give them their color.

The holes in this branching purple sponge are exhaust ports for waste water. The yellow dots are embedded anemones, distant relatives of the orange cup corals which are behind the sponge. Photo: George Lewbel.

Fishes

ANGELFISHES

You'll probably see five species of angelfishes. They are all round, disk-shaped fishes with tall, thin bodies and large vertical fins. The two largest are the **gray** (*Pomacanthus arcuatus*) and **French** (*Pomacanthus paru*) **angels**. The gray is gray with white-edged scales, while the French has yellow-edged scales. **Blue** (*Holacanthus bermudensis*) and **queen** (*Holacanthus ciliaris*) angels are somewhat smaller. Blues have blue bodies, and yellow-edged fins. Queens look like blues, but have a distinctive "crown" spot on the front of their heads. The smallest is the **rock beauty** (*Holacanthus tricolor*), a timid yellow and black fish a little larger than a big damselfish. Juvenile gray, French, blue, and queen angels have bright vertical bars. Angelfishes are often seen as mated pairs, swimming in unison around the reef.

BARRACUDA

Barracudas (*Sphyraena barracuda*) are long, silvery, torpedo-like predators. Most individuals are less than 3 feet (1 m) long, but they do grow occasionally to 6 feet (2 m). They have long jaws and large, sharp teeth, and usually travel alone. They are often curious about divers, but like to keep their distance. Although 'cudas have a bad reputation, they do not constitute a threat to divers unless harassed.

BOXFISHES AND TRUNKFISH

These fishes are covered with an armor-like layer of rigid plates. They are slow-moving bottom dwellers that sometimes find their prey in the sand by stirring it up with a jet of water from their mouths. Out on the sand, you'll often see **smooth trunkfish** (*Lactophrys triqueter*), which have blotchy black and white bodies. Over coral, **spotted trunkfish** (*Lactophrys bicaudalis*)—white with roundish black spots—and **honeycomb cowfish** (*Lactophrys polygonia*)—hexagonal spots and "cowhorn" spikes over the eyes—are more common. Although they move slowly,

boxfishes and trunkfish are in little danger from predators. They actively secrete toxins, and if placed in an aquarium, rapidly become the only living inhabitants.

BUTTERFLYFISHES

Butterflyfishes look somewhat like angelfishes, but have longer "snouts" that are used for sucking small crustaceans and other prey out of crevices. They are usually found in pairs. You're likely to see **spotfin** (*Chaetodon ocellatus*), **reef** (*Chaetodon sedentarius*), **foureye** (*Chaetodon capistratus*) and **banded** (*Chaetodon striatus*) **butterflyfishes**. The spotfin butterflyfish has a white body with yellow fins, and a black spot at the back edge of the dorsal fin. The reef butterflyfish has a wide dark vertical bar on the back of the light-colored body. The foureye butterflyfish has a black and white bull's-eye toward the rear of its body. The banded butterflyfish has several black and white vertical stripes. All four of them have a dark vertical band down the face and through the pupil of the eye. It is thought that this band makes it difficult for a predator to tell which end of the fish is the head by camouflaging the eye. This may confuse predators that normally "lead" their prey by striking forward of the head in anticipation of the prey darting ahead. The false eyespot of the foureye butterflyfish adds to the illusion, probably encouraging predators to strike toward the rear while the fish escapes in the opposite direction.

CARDINALFISHES

Cardinalfishes (family Apogonidae) are little reddish fish seen mostly at night. They have large eyes, and are less than the length of your finger. Many of them have dark spots or bands, and almost transparent bodies. They feed on plankton at night, and form the main food item for many other nocturnal predators such as sea wasps (see the section on invertebrates). During the daytime, they hide in crevices and other safe places, such as among the spines of long-spined sea urchins, or the tentacles of anemones.

Queen angelfish and blue angelfish both have bright blue bodies, but the queen is distinguished by a spotted "crown" on its head. If you remain still, queen angelfish will sometimes approach closely, but they don't like being pursued.
Photo: George Lewbel.

LIZARDS FOR LUNCH?

Along the ironshore cliffs near Karpata, you may be fortunate enough to see some of the few big iguanas left on Bonaire. They are actively hunted by the locals, who claim that the lizards taste like. . . (what else did you expect?) chicken. When little, iguanas are usually gray black, but when they get large they turn bright green. In the old days, iguanas over six feet (2 m) long were common, but nowadays, all the big ones have been turned into lunch. According to local lore, iguana meat is thought to enhance sexual prowess because male iguanas have two penises. For the record, so do many insects, but they have not been hunted with the same enthusiasm.

CHUB

Chub are silver-gray fish that form big schools above coral reefs. They are usually about a foot (30 cm) long, and have dark fins and faint, thin horizontal stripes. They are shaped like children's drawings of fishes: pointed front end, forked tail, symmetrical upper and lower halves. Chub are usually unafraid of divers, and will often swirl around them. Near hotel restaurants on the shore, very large schools of fat-looking chub can be seen waiting for diners to throw their bread in the water. There are two abundant Caribbean species—**Bermuda chub** (*Kyphosus sectatrix*) and **yellow chub** (*Kyphosus incisor*)—but they are difficult to differentiate visually.

Banded butterflyfish live on small animals that they suck out of crevices in coral heads. They are usually seen in pairs. Photo: Larry Martin.

Many species of butterflyfish, such as these foureyes, have their eyes camouflaged by vertical stripes running through the iris. Photo: George Lewbel.

DAMSELFISHES

Damselfishes include a large number of territorial little reef-bound fishes, and a few schooling forms that live above the reef. Species that are closely bound to the reef can often be found guarding a patch of algae that is carefully cultivated as a food source, or protecting a nest of eggs. These harmless but brave little fish will nip at other larger fish and divers. The most common territorial species include the **yellowtail** (*Microspathodon chrysurus*), **dusky** (*Pomacentrus fuscus*), **threespot** (*Pomacentrus planifrons*), **cocoa** (*Pomacentrus variabilis*), and **bicolor** (*Pomacentrus partitus*) **damsels**. Many damsels are dark gray and look similar, although the yellowtail (with a bright yellow tail) and the bicolor (dark front, light rear) are distinctive. **Sergeant majors** (*Abudefduf saxatilis*)—with their vertical black and white bars—are often seen in schools above the reef, or guarding large purple patches of eggs. **Blue** (*Chromis cyaneus*), and **brown** (*Chromis multilineatus*) **chromis** are also schooling fishes that feed on plankton. If you look above almost any large coral head, chances are good that you'll see a few blue chromis, and above them, a larger school of brown chromis. Blue chromis are an iridescent, electric blue color. Brown chromis are sometimes dull gray, olive-brown, or tan.

DRUMS

The drums are represented by only a few species here. However, one of them is featured in many underwater photographers' collections: the **spotted drum** (*Equetus punctatus*). This small fish has vertical black and white stripes, a black spotted nose, and a huge, fluttering dorsal fin. As it grows, white spots are added to darkening dorsal and tail fins, but younger spotted drums don't actually have any spots. Spotted drums live under overhangs and in highly eroded areas that offer good hiding places. If you approach one, it will often duck behind a coral head and re-emerge on the other side, swim back in front of the coral, and follow the same path behind the same head. If you hold your position, it will loop around as if on a track and return to the original spot in a minute or two. If you wait quietly near a spotted drum's standard route, you'll always get a chance for a second photograph.

Mature spotted drums have spots, but juvenile spotted drums have only their stripes. Photo: George Lewbel.

A sergeant-major guards its purple patch of eggs. Photo: George Lewbel.

EELS

Bonaire is famous for its moray eels.
Formerly, morays were fed to amuse tourists,
but this practice is out of fashion these days
due to numerous bites. Moray eels hide in
holes and crevices during the day, and
emerge at night to feed on sleeping fish and
crustaceans. If left alone, morays are not a
threat to divers, but they will definitely bite if
harassed. By the way, they get to define
harassment themselves, and waving food in
front of them or putting your hand or your
camera in their holes—accidentally or on
purpose—fall within their definition. With a
bit of searching, you can find **spotted**
(*Gymnothorax moringa*), **purplemouth**
(*Gymnothorax vicinus*), **goldentail** (*Muraena
miliaris*), **chain** (*Echidna catenata*) and **green**
(*Gymnothorax funebris*) **morays**. Of these,
greens are typically the most aggressive, so
keep your distance.

*Goldentail morays occupy holes in
living coral above the bottom,
rather than beneath coral heads like
most other morays. Photo: Dave
Brannon.*

*The chain moray is one of the mos
beautiful eels. Smaller than most
other morays, chained morays can
be approached closely if you move
slowly. Photo: Dave Brannon.*

Brown garden eels (*Heteroconger halis*), are thin, pencil-like beasts that group together in sand burrow colonies. Garden eels feed on plankton, bobbing their heads as they pick out their tiny food. They are usually wary of divers, and when spooked the whole colony will retract back into the sand. They are completely harmless.

Snake eels often inspire erroneous sea snake reports. They are about as big as a medium-sized terrestrial snake, and crawl along the bottom using snake-like motions to follow cracks and other bottom contours. They have little tubular nostrils, and very small teeth. They cannot hurt divers, since they feed on tiny crustaceans. **Sharptail** (*Myrichthys acuminatus*) and **goldspotted** (*Myrichthys oculatus*) **snake eels** are most often seen on coral-covered slopes.

FROGFISHES

Frogfishes (family Antennariidae) are camouflaged, globular beasts with a wiggling filament (the "lure") protruding from their snouts, immediately above large upward-facing mouths. They are bottom dwellers who wait for unsuspecting prey to be attracted by their lure. Most frogfish around Bonaire are orange colored, and usually seen on sponges.

GOATFISHES

Goatfishes have long sensors called "barbels" protruding from their chins which are used to seek out food in soft bottom areas. They often travel in large schools. A school of goatfishes can really churn up a sand flat when feeding. There are two common species. **Spotted goatfish** (*Pseudupeneus maculatus*) have three rectangular spots on their sides. **Yellow goatfish** (*Mulloidichthys martinicus*) have a yellow line that runs along their sides, and a yellow tail. Yellow goatfish frequently school with yellowtail snappers.

GROUPERS, SEABASSES AND BASSLETS

There are many kinds of groupers and seabasses, and some of them are quite difficult to tell apart in the field due to similar body shapes and rapid color changes. They generally have large mouths and large, fan-shaped tails used to rush and engulf smaller fishes. They tend to be shy if approached by divers. Their behavior can be aptly described as "lurking." Around Bonaire and Klein, you're likely to find many **coneys** (*Epinephelus fulvus*), **rock hinds** (*Epinephelus adscensionis*) and **red hinds** (*Epinephelus guttatus*), **graysbys** (*Epinephelus cruentatus*) and **tiger groupers** (*Mycteroperca tigris*). Of these, only the tiger grouper typically exceeds about 2 feet (61 cm) in length. The **Nassau grouper** (*Epinephelus striatus*), which is very common in the northern Caribbean, is uncommon here.

Coneys are usually either dark brown or distinctively dark above and pale below, though they sometimes turn bright yellow. They have two black spots on their chin and two black spots just forward of their tail. Rock and red hinds and graysbys are reddish-brown, spotted fishes rather similar in appearance; tiger groupers have distinctive vertical bars.

Within the same large taxonomic group are a number of timid, closely related, much smaller fishes often overlooked by divers. Above sandy patches, look for **harlequin bass** (*Serranus tigrinus*) with yellow and black bars, and the tan **tobaccofish** (*Serranus tabacarius*) with white blotches on the back. Beneath overhangs, look for purple and yellow **fairy basslets** (*Gramma loreto*), and also **blackcap basslets** (*Gramma melacara*) which are purple with dark "cap" on the head. Basslets often suspend themselves upside-down. Finally, note the large schools of **creolefish** (*Paranthias furcifer*) that cruise along the seaward edges of the shelves. Creolefish are reddish-purple, and often carry large gray, alien-looking, parasitic isopod crustaceans attached to their gill covers. These parasites undoubtedly slow their hosts down, but probably don't cause enough tissue damage to be fatal. Individuals carrying even two isopods seem to have normal activity patterns.

Coneys come in several background color patterns, including red with many spots, red-and-white two-tone with many spots, and yellow with few spots. No matter what color they are, coneys nearly always show two dark dots on their lower lips. Photos: George Lewbel.

Fairy basslets, also called "royal gramma," are usually found hovering upside-down beneath ledges, as well as near orange elephant-ear sponges. Photo: George Lewbel.

GRUNTS AND SNAPPERS

Grunts and snappers are similar-shaped fishes with streamlined, rather symmetrical bodies, sloping foreheads, and large mouths. Most of them are less than two feet (60 cm) long. Grunts can make loud sounds, both underwater and when captured above water. They form large schools near the edges of coral reefs during the daytime, and disperse at night to feed on small crustaceans and other prey. It's hard to differentiate between grunts and snappers visually, although grunts tend to have brighter colors. Snappers have pronounced canine teeth, but these are not visible unless a fish has its mouth open.

You're likely to see **bluestriped grunts** (*Haemulon sciurus*) which have yellow and blue horizontal lines, a black tail and dorsal; **French grunts** (*Haemulon flavolineatum*) with their horizontal and diagonal lines of yellow, blue or brown; **smallmouth grunts** (*Haemulon chrysargyreum*), similar to the French grunt, but with horizontal lines only; **white grunts** (*Haemulon plumieri*) which have blue and yellow stripes on the face, and a light checkered pattern on the rest of the body; **sailor's choice** (*Haemulon parrai*) with dark fins and a gray body; and **black margates** (*Anisotremus surinamensis*) with a big black spot in the lower center of their tall body.

The most common snappers in this area are **yellowtail snappers** (*Ocyurus chrysurus*) which have a bluish-silver body, wide horizontal yellow line, and yellow fins and tail; **mahogany snappers** (*Lutjanus mahogoni*) with large yellowish eyes, and the maroon-colored edges on their fins and tail; and **schoolmaster snappers** (*Lutjanus apodus*) which have bright yellow fins and faint vertical bars. Mahogany snappers usually group in schools, as do smaller schoolmaster and yellowtail snappers. Yellowtail snappers and yellow goatfish frequently school together. Larger schoolmasters are often seen singly.

JACKS

Jacks are sleek, fast-swimming predators. They are usually silvery on their sides with darker backs, and have a deeply forked tail. **Bar jacks** (*Caranx ruber*) are most often seen near reefs. They have bluish-silver bodies, and a dark line that runs from the dorsal fin down onto the lower half of the tail. Bar jacks sometimes follow other fishes very closely, perhaps hoping to share a meal or sneak up on their own prey. **Horse-eye jacks** (*Caranx latus*) are sometimes seen near the edges of drop-offs or near piers, circling divers in small schools. They are large, silvery fishes with big black eyes and yellow tails.

LIZARDFISH

Lizardfish are small, lurk-and-lunge predators that sit quietly on the bottom until other, smaller fish swim by. Then, they dart upward and seize their prey. They are cigar-shaped, with tiny needle-like teeth. They generally adopt mottled dark and light patterns, and sometimes rest partially buried in sand. The **sand diver** (*Synodus intermedius*) is the most common lizardfish around Bonaire and Klein.

An isopod crustacean clings to the gill cover of a creolefish. Creolefish often carry these external parasites. The isopod may remain in place for the life of the fish. Photo: George Lewbel.

A bluestriped grunt at a cleaning station has its mouth and gill covers open so that gobies and other cleaner fishes can enter and remove parasites. Photo: George Lewbel.

Flounders

The most common representative of this group is the **peacock flounder** (*Bothus lunatus*). It has a flattened body with both eyes on the "top" (really its left side, but the right eye has migrated around the head). The peacock flounder is usually about a foot (30 cm) long, and has a conspicuous pectoral fin which is the one next to the gill cover. It is often sand-colored, since it lives on the bottom and can change its color to match its surroundings, but has beautiful bright blue rings on its body.

Needlefishes

Needlefishes are very thin, long, silvery fishes that linger just below the surface of the water. They are highly reflective, and blend into the surface film, making them difficult for their prey (other small fishes) to see from below. They have needle-like "beaks," and swim with horizontal undulating motions, a bit like snakes. There are a number of species of needlefishes, all of which can be hard to identify. Most are less than a foot (30 cm) long, though one species, the **houndfish** (*Tylosurus crocodilus*), does grow larger than three feet (1 m).

Parrotfishes

Parrotfishes can be recognized by their parrotlike beak, which is formed by the fusion of their upper and lower teeth. Crunching noisily—divers can actually hear them—parrotfishes feed on coral and algae-encrusted rocks during the day. At night, they sleep wrapped in a protective mucus cocoon. Much of the white sediment between coral heads consists of undigested bits of coral that have passed through the guts of parrotfishes.

There are many species of parrotfishes, and identification of smaller individuals can be very difficult. Most (or perhaps all) parrotfishes undergo one or more sex changes as they age. Large males are fairly distinctive, however. You'll easily recognize **queen parrotfish** (*Scarus vetula*) because of the blue stripes around the eyes and mouth; **rainbow parrotfish** (*Scarus guacamaia*), which are a brilliant green on the rear of the body and

pinkish in front; and **blue parrotfish** (*Scarus coeruleus*) with their uniform blue color. **Midnight parrotfish** (*Scarus coelestinus*) have a dark blue body with light blue spots on the head. **Stoplight parrotfish** (*Sparisoma viride*) have a red belly, and brown and white scales in one color phase. In another color phase they have a blue-green body with a yellow spot at the tip of the gill cover and the base of the tail.

Puffers and Porcupinefishes

Most puffers can swallow water and swell up, making them less attractive to predators. This is extremely defensive behavior—a last-ditch effort to avoid being eaten—and puffers should never be captured and held by divers as an amusement. The **sharpnose puffer** (*Canthigaster rostrata*) is about the size of a regulator first stage, and hides among gorgonians. It has a pointed snout, and a bulbous, smooth-skinned brown and white body with blue markings. The **balloonfish** (*Diodon holocanthus*) has a blotched brown and tan body, and is usually less than a foot (30 cm) long. The spines on its head are longer than on the rest of the body, and its eyes have beautiful iridescent turquoise spots within the pupil. The **porcupinefish** (*Diodon hystrix*) grows up to three feet (1 m) in length, and has a grayish body with little black spots.

Rays

Rays are usually either shaped like a diamond or a disk, and can often be found lying on the bottom partially camouflaged by sand. Their eyes are on the top of their bodies, and most have a long tail with a sting near the base. This spike is venomous, but stingrays use it only in self-defense. The **yellow stingray** (*Urolophus jamaicensis*) has a yellowish mottled round disk and is usually about a foot (30 cm) in diameter. It frequents sand flats and other soft-sediment areas, and is sometimes partially buried, so look carefully before you touch down on a sandy bottom. The **southern stingray** (*Dasyatis americana*) is diamond-shaped, and grows up to six feet (2 m) across. Southern stingrays are fairly timid and difficult to approach closely.

There are two large rays sometimes seen near the edges of drop-offs, especially near Klein or at the northern end of Bonaire. **Spotted eagle rays** (*Aetobatus narinari*) have dark bodies with white spots on top, and their wingspan may exceed six feet (2 m). **Atlantic mantas** (*Manta birostris*) are even larger, reaching 20 feet (6 m), and have big mouths and large flaps on either side of the mouth. Both are harmless to divers. If you remain motionless, either of these two rays may come closer for a look.

SCORPIONFISHES

Scorpionfishes are well-camouflaged, rock-like beasts that rest motionless on the bottom, waiting for something smaller to mistake them for terrain. They have poisonous dorsal spines, and they tend not to move unless forced to. As a result, divers sometimes come to rest on them, with very painful consequences for the diver. The most common species around Bonaire is the **spotted scorpionfish** (*Scorpaena plumieri*). It is usually about a foot (30 cm) long, and covered with fine filaments, brown or red spots, and white blotches. To avoid meeting one by accident, watch your buoyancy control, and don't touch anything that looks like a brown rock, especially if it has eyes!

A queen parrotfish with a moustache of algae growing on its "beak."
Photo: George Lewbel.

The balloonfish can erect its spines and inflate itself with water when threatened. Please don't grab these shy, comical animals, forcing them to inflate out of fear. Photo: George Lewbel.

121

SEA HORSES

Sea horses (family Syngnathidae) are usually found in shallow water, clinging to gorgonians or staghorn coral with prehensile tails. Male sea horses carry their young around in pouches, giving them a bulbous, pregnant look. Sea horses are typically yellow or yellow and brown in this area. They prefer to remain in the same general location over long periods of time. If you tell your dive guide that you'd like to see sea horses, chances are good that he or she will know exactly where to find them. Sea horses are very fragile. Please look, but don't touch them or chase them away from their home turf.

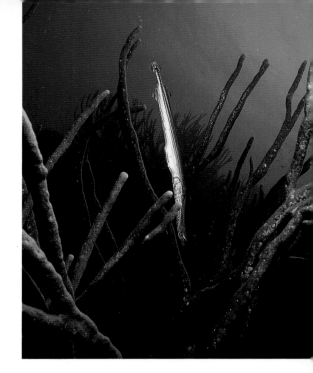

SQUIRRELFISHES

Usually five to eight inches (13–20 cm) in length, squirrelfishes have fairly prominent dorsal fin spines. Their bodies tend to be reddish in color. As you can tell by their large eyes, they are typically nocturnal. There are about half a dozen species, which are fairly difficult to tell apart. The most distinctive one is the **blackbar soldierfish** (*Myripristis jacobus*), which has a bright red body and a vertical black bar along the edge of the gill cover.

Trumpetfish like to hang vertically among gorgonian stalks or sponges. There is only one Caribbean species, which can appear brown, yellow, silver or even greenish. Photo: George Lewbel.

Note the small cleaner shrimps on the head of this squirrelfish. Photo: George Lewbel.

SURGEONFISHES

Surgeonfishes are oval-shaped, tall, thin fishes that have a contrasting spot at the base of the tail. The spot is a modified spine used for self-defense. The sharp spine is normally kept sheathed, but can unfold outward to deter predators.

You're likely to see **ocean surgeonfish** (*Acanthurus bahianus*) and **doctorfish** (*Acanthurus chirurgus*), either singly or in small groups, and big schools of **blue tang** (*Acanthurus coeruleus*). Ocean surgeonfish and doctorfish are often tan-colored, but can change from slate gray to dark blue in an instant. Both have mascara-like markings around their eyes, but the doctorfish has vertical bars and the ocean surgeonfish does not. Adult blue tang range from light blue to indigo, although juveniles are brilliant yellow. Blue tang often feed in huge mobs, overwhelming the best defenses of damselfishes in order to graze on their gardens.

TARPON

This impressive large fish is silvery in color with a darker greenish or bluish back, and huge reflective scales. **Tarpon** (*Megalops atlanticus*) can grow to about eight feet (2.4 m) in length. They often are seen at night when they are attracted to dock lights and come into the shallows.

TILEFISH

Sand tilefish (*Malacanthus plumieri*) are slender, graceful, whitish fish up to two feet (60 cm) long, with rippling dorsal and ventral fins. They usually hover just above the sand. When threatened, they dart head- or tail-first into their burrows. The burrows are surrounded by dead coral chunks brought there by the fish. Sometimes these "nests" can be over ten feet (3 m) in diameter.

TRIGGERFISHES AND FILEFISHES

Triggerfishes and filefishes are closely related groups that have a number of features in common. They have a long, sharp spine forward of their dorsal fins. This spine can be raised erect when danger threatens. Triggerfishes have a second spine that locks the primary spine in an upright position when needed. Filefishes have such rough scales that their skins were used in olden times as natural sandpaper or files (hence the name of the group). Both triggerfishes and filefishes swim in a clumsy-looking fashion, flapping their dorsal and anal (lower) fins to scull, rather than using their tails.

The most abundant members of this group include the **black durgon** (*Melichthys niger*), which has a black body with white edges along its dorsal and anal fins; and the **scrawled filefish** (*Aluterus scriptus*), which has a long ungainly body with blue spots and a broad tail. If you're lucky, you may see a **queen triggerfish** (*Balistes vetula*), which has a diamond-shaped bluish body, light blue stripes on the face, and long trailing fin tips. Along drop-offs, look seaward; you might spot an **ocean triggerfish** (*Canthidermis sufflamen*), a large gray-colored trigger with a black spot at the base of the pectoral fin near the gill cover.

TRUMPETFISH AND CORNETFISH

Both of these two fishes are long and very skinny. The **trumpetfish** (*Aulostomus maculatus*) is usually silver or tan with darker blotches and spots, but can turn brown or even bright yellow. It reaches a size of about three feet (1 m), and often hovers vertically among gorgonians. It specializes in darting suddenly forward and engulfing smaller fishes. **Cornetfish** (*Fistularia tabacaria*) are similarly slender, but reach a length of six feet (2 m). They are generally olive-colored, and have bright blue spots and a long filament at the tip of their tails. You usually see them swimming just barely above the bottom by themselves, but they sometimes form large mating aggregations.

WRASSES AND HOGFISHES

Usually less than a foot long (30 cm) at maturity, members of the wrasse family can often be recognized by their protruding buck teeth. Wrasses are closely related to parrotfishes and hogfishes, all of which usually swim with a rather jerky motion, using their pectoral fins (those just behind the gill covers) to "row" their way through the water. Smaller wrasses are cigar-shaped. You usually see wrasses rooting around in sand flats, or hovering in small harems above coral heads.

Wrasses go through sex changes over their life spans. Smaller, black and white individuals are often females or immature males; brightly-colored individuals are often sexually mature males. It's usually possible to identify large males by species, but younger wrasses look very similar to one another. Those most easily recognized include the **bluehead wrasse** (*Thalassoma bifasciatum*) which has a blue head, and black and white bands near the head; the **yellowhead wrasse** (*Halichoeres garnoti*) with a yellow head and a single dark band around the middle of the body; and the **puddingwife** (*Halichoeres radiatus*) which has a blue-green body, yellow-edged tail and often exceeds one foot (30 cm).

There is one wrasse that forms large schools in mid-water. The **creole wrasse** (*Clepticus parrai*) has a purple or dark blue body with a black spot on the nose between the eyes. It frequently swims with creolefish (see Groupers and Seabasses).

Hogfish (*Lachnolaimus maximus*) are unusual, tall-bodied tan fishes with three long spines on the front of the dorsal fin. They reach three feet (1 m) in length, and are easy to approach. Their relatives, the **Spanish hogfish** (*Bodianus rufus*), are more common around Bonaire. Some Spanish hogfish have distinctive two-tone coloration, with purple on the upper parts of their bodies, and yellow on the lower. However, mottled purple or blue Spanish hogfish are often seen. They sometimes feed on urchins, and can take apart a long-spined black urchin faster than you can set the f-stop on a Nikonos. If you stir up a sandy bottom, they'll come over to see if they can find a few uncovered crustaceans.

Spanish hogfish adults feed on such challenging items as long-spined urchins. Juveniles sometimes staff cleaning stations, helping gobies remove parasites from larger fish. Photo: George Lewbel.

APPENDIX 1

EMERGENCY NUMBERS

Bonaire Police/Ambulance/Chamber   8000
Divers Alert Network (DAN)   (919) 684–8111

Both a hospital and a hyperbaric recompression facility are available on Bonaire. Even larger medical facilities are only a short flight away on Bonaire's island neighbor, Curaçao.

Almost all the dive guides on the island are trained to respond to an emergency, and almost all the boats carry oxygen and first aid equipment. You can access emergency assistance on Bonaire by calling the telephone number 8000. This is similar to calling 911 in the United States. Through this single number you can activate ambulance, police and recompression chamber personnel.

Once you are in the emergency medical system you can have the medical personnel consult with the Diver's Alert Network (DAN) if you have a diving injury. This way you will not waste valuable time before initiating treatment and can still call on the expertise of DAN's hyperbaric doctors.

When contacting an emergency number, be sure to state your name, exact location and the nature of the emergency. Stay on the phone until the operator confirms that all the information has been received correctly. Stay on the scene to give the responding unit additional information and assistance.

Divers Alert Network (DAN)

The Divers Alert Network (DAN), a non-profit membership organization affiliated with Duke University Medical Center, operates a 24-hour emergency number **(919) 684-8111** (emergencies only) to provide divers and physicians with medical advice on treating diving injuries. DAN can also organize air evacuation to a recompression chamber.

Since many emergency room physicians do not know how to properly treat diving injuries, it is highly recommended that in the event of an accident, you have the physician consult a DAN doctor specializing in diving medicine.

All DAN members receive $100,000 emergency medical evacuation assistance and a subscription to the dive safety magazine, *Alert Diver*. New members receive the DAN *Dive and Travel Medical Guide* and can buy up to $125,000 of dive accident insurance.

DAN offers emergency oxygen first-aid training, and provides funding and consulting for recompression chambers worldwide. They also conduct diving research at Duke University's F.G. Hall Hyperbaric Center.

DAN's address is The Peter B. Bennett Center, 6 West Colony Place, Durham, NC 27705. Their non-emergency medical information number is (919) 684-2948. To join call (800) 446-2671.

APPENDIX 2

USEFUL NUMBERS FOR VISITORS

Bonaire Tourism Offices

An up-to-date rate sheet of Bonaire's resorts is available at one of the offices of the Bonaire Department of Tourism listed below.

United States

10 Rockefeller Plaza, Suite 900
New York, NY 10020
(212) 956-5911
(800) 826-6247

Canada

815-A Queen Street East
Toronto, Ontario M4M 1H8
(416) 465-2958

Aruba

Aruba Fiesta Gallery
Havenstraat #5, Second Floor
Aruba, Dutch West Indies
2978-35378

Bonaire

Kaya Simon Bolivar #12
Kralendijk, Bonaire
Netherlands Antilles
011-599-7-8322 or 8649

Holland

Antillenhuis
Badhuisweg 173-175
2597 JP Den Haag
Netherlands
011-31-70-512811

Venezuela

Torre Capriles
Piso 2
Oficinia #202, Plaza Venezuela
Caracas, Venezuela
723460 or 723583

West Germany

Spaldingstrasse 1
2000 Hamburg 1
West Germany
011-40-1-230967

Car Rental Companies

A.B. Car Rental

Flamingo Airport
8980, 8667

Avis Rent-A-Car

Boulevard J.A. Abraham
Kralendijk
5795, 8922

Budget Rent-A-Car

Kaya L.D. Gerharts #22
P.O. Box 115
Kralendijk
8300 ext. 225/229/242
Airport: 8315, 8300 ext. 235
U.S. (800) 344-4439

Dollar Rent-A-Car

Kaya Gob. N. Debrot
Kralendijk
8888

Flamingo Car Rental

(Flamingo Tours N.V.)
P.O. Box 156
Kralendijk
8313 (airport)

Sunray Car Rental

P.O. Box 217
Kralendijk
8600 ext. 34

Appendix 3

Resorts and Scuba Diving Centers

To telephone Bonaire from the United States add **011-599-7** before the four-digit local number.

Black Durgon Inn & Bonaire Scuba Center

P.O. Box 106
Kralendijk
Bonaire, N.A.
8978
Fax: 8846

U.S. Contact:

Bonaire Tours
11143 NW 7th #104
Miami, FL 33172
(800) 526-2370
Fax: (305) 229-1433

Buddy Beach & Dive Resort & Buddy Watersports

P.O. Box 231
Kralendijk
Bonaire, N.A.
5080
Fax: 8647

U.S. Contact:

Rothschild Travel Consultants
900 West End Avenue, Suite B
New York, NY 10025
(800) 359-0747
(212) 662-4858
Fax: (212) 749-6172

Captain Don's Habitat & Habitat Dive Center

P.O. Box 88
Kralendijk
Bonaire, N.A.
8290
Fax: 8240

U.S. Contact:

Habitat North American Office
903 South American Way
Miami, FL 33132
(800) 327-6709
Fax: (305) 371-2337

Carib Inn & Carib Inn Dive Shop

P.O. Box 68
Kralendijk
Bonaire, N.A.
8819
Fax: 5295

U.S. Contact: none

Divi Flamingo Beach Resort & Casino & Peter Hughes Dive Bonaire

P.O. Box 143
Kralendijk
Bonaire, N.A.
8285
Fax: 8238

U.S. Contact:

Divi Hotels Marketing Inc.
6340 Quadrangle Drive #300
Chapel Hill, NC 27514
(919) 419-3484/2075

Harbour Village Beach Resort & Great Adventure Bonaire

Kaya Gobernador Debrot
Bonaire, N.A.
7500
Fax: 7507

U.S. Contact:

First Class Resorts
One Alhambra Plaza, Suite 1150
Coral Gables, FL 33134
(800) 424-0004

Lions Dive Hotel Bonaire & Bon Bini Divers

Kaya Gobernador N.
Ddbrot 90
Kralendijk
Bonaire, N.A.
5580
Fax: 5680

U.S. Contact:

Caribbean Dive Tours
732 Johnson Ferry Road #106
Marietta, GA 30068
(800) 786-3483

Sand Dollar Beach Club & Sand Dollar Dive and Photo

P.O. Box 175
Kralendijk
Bonaire, N.A.
8783
Fax: 8760

U.S. Contact:

Caradonna Caribbean Tours
P.O. Box 3299
Longwood, FL 32779
(800) 288-4773

Sunset Beach Hotel

P.O. Box 333
Kralendijk
Bonaire, N.A.
(800) 354-8142 (Bonaire direct)
8448/8291
Fax: 8118/8593

U.S. Contact:

Caradonna Caribbean Tours
P.O. Box 3299
Longwood, FL 32779
(800) 288-4773

Bonaire Sunset Travel
13876 SW 56th, Suite 188
Miami, FL 33175
(800) 344-4439

Sunset Beach Inn/Villas

P.O. Box 115
Kralendijk
Bonaire, N.A.
8291/8448
Fax: 8865

U.S. Contact:

Caradonna Caribbean Tours
P.O. Box 3299
Longwood, FL 32779
(800) 288-4773

Bonaire Sunset Travel
13876 SW 56th, Suite 188
Miami, FL 33175
(800) 344-4439

Plaza Resort Bonaire & Toucan Diving

Abraham Boulevard 80
Kralendijk
Bonaie, N.A.
2500
Fax: 7133

U.S. Contact:

Travel Marketing Services Ltd.
343 Neponset Street
Canton, MA 02021
(800) 766-6016

INDEPENDENT DIVE OPERATIONS

Blue Divers

Kaya Den Teraz
Kralendijk
Bonaire, N.A.
6860
Fax: 6865

U.S. Contact:

Great Southern Island Adventures
416 E. Amite Street
Jackson, MS 39201
(800) 748-8733

Dee Scarr's "Touch the Sea"

P.O. Box 369
Kralendijk
Bonaire, N.A.
8529

U.S. Contact: none

Dive Inn Bonaire

Kaya C.E.B. Hellmund 27
Kralendijk
Bonaire, N.A.
8761
Fax: 8513
Locations at Sunset Beach Hotel, Sunset Inn
and Bonaire Caribbean Club

U.S. Contact: none

INDEX

A **boldface** page number denotes a picture caption.
An <u>underlined</u> page number indicates detailed treatment.

Anemones, **18**, **30**, 59, 63-65, 84, 88, 94, <u>96-97</u>, **96**, **98**, <u>102</u>, **111**
Angelfishes, 36, 56, 62, 66-67, 84, 90, **110**, <u>112</u>, **113**
Arawak Indians, 10
Barham, HMS, 46
Barracuda, 34, 53, 54, **57**, 57, 64, <u>112</u>
Basket stars, 55, <u>104</u>
Basslets, 36, 70, <u>117</u>, **118**
Boat diving, <u>38</u>
Boca Onima, **41**
Bon Bini Divers, <u>22</u>
Bonaire Marine Park, 36-38, 80
Bonaire Scuba Center, <u>21</u>, 27
Brandaris Hill, 10, 12
Brittle star, **96**, <u>104</u>
Buddy Dive, <u>21</u>
Butterflyfishes, 36, <u>112</u>, **114**
Cardinalfish, <u>112</u>
Christmas tree worms, **44**, <u>103</u>
Chromis, 36, 62, 76, 78, 84-85
Climate, <u>14</u>
Conch, **33**, <u>33</u>, 34, 36, 55, <u>108</u>
Coneys, 36, 57, 90, <u>117</u>, **118**
Corals, <u>97-99</u>
    Cavernous star, 34, 68, 75, 78, 90
    Black, 63-64, 68, 70, 75, 78-82, 86, 88, 90, 92, <u>101</u>
    Brain, 34, 54, 62, **80**, 80, **93**
    Elkhorn, 34, 44, 48, 56, 62-66, 71, 86, 88-90
    Fire, 34, 51, 53, 55-56, 62-64, 84-86, 88-90, 93, **100**
    Flower, 36
    Gorgonians, 34, 36, 44, 46-48, 50, 54, 56, 64, 66-68, 70, 76, 79, 84, 84, <u>101</u>
    Mountainous star, 34, 52-53, 66, 68, 76-79, 81-82, 85, 89-90, **99**
    Orange cup, **10**, 50, 58, **59**, 66, 68, 82, 88, **111**
    Pencil, 36, 68, 75, 89
    Pillar, 34, 60, 63

Plate, **20**, 62, 64-68, 70-71, **74**, 75, **77**, 78-79, 81-82, 84-86, 89-90, **91**
Sea fans, **20**, 51, 53, 55, 74, 82, 86, <u>101</u>
Sheet, **27**, 36, 64
Staghorn, 34, 48, 51, 54, 56, 63-64, 66, 84-86, 88-90
Wire, 63-64, 68, 70, **77**, 78, 84, 86, 88-89, **93**
Corallimorpharians, **18**
Cornetfish, 53, 60, **61**, <u>123</u>
Crabs, 36, **40**, 58, 74, <u>105-106</u>
Crinoid, **56**, 63, 85, <u>104</u>
Currency, <u>14</u>
Damselfishes, 34, 53, 62, 84, 89-90, <u>114</u>, **115**
Depths, <u>37</u>
Dive Bonaire, <u>23</u>, 57
Dive Inn, <u>27</u>
Dive sites
    Alice in Wonderland, <u>51</u>, **54**
    Angel City, <u>51</u>, **54**
    Barcadera, <u>65</u>
    Bari Reef, <u>62-63</u>
    Bloodlet, <u>68</u>
    Boca Bartol, 34, 38, 41, <u>73</u>, **74**
    Boca Dreifi (Chet's Cove), <u>93</u>
    Bonaventure, <u>75</u>
    Bonheur de Betsy (Rock Pile), <u>76-77</u>
    Calabas Reef, <u>57</u>
    Captain Don's Reef, <u>78</u>
    Carl's Hill (Punta P'abou), 34, <u>88</u>
    Carl's Hill Annex (Aggressor III), <u>27</u>, <u>86</u>
    Chez Hines, <u>55</u>
    Cliff (Flagpole), 34, <u>63-64</u>
    Corporal Meiss, **56**
    Debbie Bob, <u>55</u>
    Ebo's Reef, <u>92</u>
    Forest, <u>81</u>
    Front Porch, <u>60</u>
    Hands-Off, <u>80</u>
    Hilma Hooker, <u>52-53</u>, **53**

Jeanne's Glory, **50**
Jerry's Jam (Ebo's Special), <u>89</u>
Joanne's Sunchi, <u>77</u>
Just-a-nice-dive (Kanal), <u>74-75</u>
Karpata, 34, 38, **70**, <u>71</u>, 113
Knife, <u>90</u>
La Dania's Leap, 38, <u>69-70</u>
Lake (Lake Bowker), <u>53</u>, **54**
La Machaca, <u>63</u>
Leonora's Reef, <u>89</u>
Lighthouse (Willemstoren), 38, 41, <u>44</u>, **46**
Mi Dushi (Johanna's Revenge), <u>86</u>
Monte's Divi (Divi Tree), <u>76</u>
Munk's Haven, <u>82</u>
Oil Slick Leap, **30**, <u>66</u>
Ol' Blue, <u>67</u>
Petrie's Pillar, <u>65</u>
Pink Beach (Witte Pan, Cabaje), <u>47</u>
Playa Benge, 38, 41, <u>71</u>
Playa Frans, <u>93</u>
Punt Vierkant, 38, <u>54</u>
RSD (Ricky-Sue-Dave), <u>92</u>
Rappel, 34, <u>68</u>
Red Slave (Rode Pan, Pietike, Pelike), 38, 41, <u>46</u>, 47
Salt City (Invisibles, Salina Abou), <u>47-48</u>
Salt Pier, **48**, <u>48-50</u>, **49**, 59
Sampler, <u>90</u>
Sharon's Serenity, <u>84</u>
Small Wall, <u>64</u>
Something Special (Playa P'abou), **60**, **61**
South Bay, <u>78</u>
Southwest Corner, <u>82</u>, **83**
Thousand Steps (Piedra Haltu), 38, <u>66</u>
Town Pier, **10**, **18**, 41, 50, <u>58-59</u>, **59**
Twixt, <u>84</u>
Valerie's Hill, <u>85</u>
Windsock Steep, <u>56</u>
Divers Alert Network, <u>125</u>

Dolphins, bottlenose, 84
Drums, spotted, 36, 57, 88, **115**
Durgon, black, 78, <u>123</u>
Eels, <u>116-117</u>
    Chain, **116**
    Garden, 36, 48, 51, 54-55,
       57, 60, **61**, 62-64
    Goldentail, **116**
    Green moray, **22**, 63, 68, 90
    Morays, 36, 57, 59, 60, 66,
       92
    Snake, 60, 62-63
    Spotted, 68, **69**, 90
Electricity, <u>14</u>
Emergency numbers, <u>125</u>
Fan worms, **13**, **78**
Filefishes, 59, 65, 79, 81, 92,
    <u>123</u>
Fire worms, 64, 89, **103**
First aid, <u>106-107</u>
Flamingo, pink, 12, 38, <u>111</u>
Flamingo tongue, **34**, <u>108</u>
Flounders, peacock, 34, 47, 57,
    62, 63, 74-77, <u>120</u>
Frogfish, <u>117</u>
Goatfishes, 34, 55, 57, 60, 64,
    76-77, 90, <u>117</u>
Great Adventures Bonaire, <u>24</u>
Groupers, 46, 56-57, 73-74, 92,
    <u>117</u>
    Nassau, 36, 54
    Tiger, 51, 53-54, **54**, 55-56,
       66, 77, 89
Grunts, 36, 63, 73, 76, <u>118-119</u>
Hazardous marine life, <u>101</u>
Hinds, 36- 56-57, 63, 90, <u>117</u>
Hogfish, Spanish, 36, 66-67, 86,
    90, **124**
Hydroids, stinging, **90**, <u>100</u>
Jacks, 44, 48, 81, <u>119</u>
    Bar, 34, 55, 74, 77
    Horse-eye, 52, 55, 74, 79
Jawfish, yellow-headed, 47, 57,
    60
Jellyfish, <u>102</u>
Kralendijk, 12, <u>13</u>, 17, 20
Lac Bay, **33**, 33
Language, <u>15</u>
Lizardfishes, 34, 37, 51, 60, 64,
    75-76, **76**, <u>119</u>
Lobsters, 60, 62, <u>108</u>
Map, 42-43
Mojarras, 34, 60, 77

Moorings, 36, <u>37</u>
Mullet, 34, 56-57, 60, 63, 74
Needlefish, <u>120</u>
Nudibranchs, 63, 85, 89, **109**
Obelisks, <u>47</u>, **49**
Octopus, 64, **110**
Parrotfishes, 34, 52-53, 55-56,
    62, 64, 74, 76, 84-86, 90,
    <u>120</u>, **120**
Photo Bonaire, <u>24</u>
Photo Tours, <u>23</u>
Portuguese Man-of-War, <u>101</u>
Prisca's Ice Cream, **72**
Puffers, cover, 34, 58, 64, <u>120</u>,
    121
Rays, 36, 60, 63, 73-74, 77,
    <u>120-121</u>
Resorts
    Black Durgon Inn, <u>21</u>, 64
    Buddy Dive Resort, <u>21</u>
    Captain Don's Habitat, <u>21</u>-
      22, 63-64, 75
    Carib Inn, <u>22</u>
    Divi Flamingo Beach Resort,
      <u>22-23</u>, 57
    Harbour Village Beach
      Resort, <u>23-24</u>
    Lions Dive Hotel Bonaire, <u>24</u>
    Plaza Resort Bonaire, <u>26-27</u>
    Sand Dollar Beach Club, <u>24</u>-
      <u>25</u>, 62
    Sunset Beach Hotel, <u>25</u>, **26**,
      92
    Sunset Beach Inn/Villas, <u>25</u>-
      <u>26</u>
Restaurants
    Beefeater, <u>28</u>
    Capricorn, <u>32</u>
    China Garden, <u>28</u>
    Cozzoli's Pizzeria, <u>30</u>
    Calabas, <u>28</u>
    Chibi Chibi, <u>30</u>
    Green Parrot, <u>31</u>
    Kasa Coral, <u>31</u>
    Lac Snack, <u>33</u>
    Oasis, <u>31</u>
    Playa Lechi, <u>31</u>
    Raffles, <u>31-32</u>
    Rendez Vous, <u>32</u>
    Rum Runners, <u>32</u>
Salt, 10, 12, **49**
Sand Dollar Dive and Photo, <u>25</u>
Scorpionfish, 60, **61**, 63, <u>121</u>

Sea cucumber, <u>104</u>
Sea horse, **8**, 86, <u>122</u>
Sea stars, **85**, <u>103</u>
Sea urchins, 85, <u>103-104</u>, **104**
Shark, hammerhead, 73
Sharksuckers, **81**
Shopping, <u>17</u>
Shore diving, <u>38</u>
Shore markers, <u>37</u>
Shrimp, 62, <u>106-108</u>, **122**
Snappers, 34, 36, 52, 55, 73-74,
    84, <u>118-119</u>, **119**
Snorkeling, 31, <u>39</u>, **39**, 48, 53,
    55-56, 62, 64
Sponges, **12**, 40, 44, 46-47, **88**,
    91, <u>94</u>, 96
    Barrel, 36, 50, **56**, 62, 82, **83**,
      94
    Basket, 54, 56
    Elephant-ear, 55, 77-81, 85-
      86, **118**
    Finger (linguini), **50**, 50, 67,
      76, 86, 89
    Fluorescent, 82, **83**, 94
    Orange, 82, 84, 92
    Purple tube, **17**, **50**, 51, 59,
      62, 85-86, **87**, 88, **111**
Squid, 73, <u>110</u>
Squirrelfishes, 36, **122**
Surgeonfishes, **2-3**, 50, 57, <u>123</u>
Sunset Beach Dive Center, <u>25</u>
Tarpon, **48**, 57, 59, 62, 74, <u>123</u>
Telephone, <u>17</u>
Temperature
    Air, <u>14</u>
    Water, <u>36</u>
Tilefish, sand, 34, 36, 48, 64,
    77, <u>123</u>
Tobaccofish, 34, 84, <u>117</u>
Toucan Diving, <u>27</u>
Touch the Sea, 22, <u>75</u>
Triggerfish, 79, <u>123</u>
Trumpetfishes, 53, 57, 59, **61**,
    76, 83-84, **122**, <u>123</u>
Trunkfishes, 34, 62, 77, <u>112</u>
Turtle, 72, **81**
Undersea Adventures, <u>23</u>
Vespucci, Amerigo, 10
Visibility, <u>36-37</u>
Washington/Slagbaai National
    Park, 12, 17, 71, **72**, 73
Windward diving, <u>39</u>
Wrasses, 34, 62-64, <u>124</u>